The Secret
Survival Manual
✗ ✗

Other books by J. Brent Bill

Cruisin' and Choosin'
Lunch Is My Favorite Subject
Rock and Roll, Revised
Stuff Your Guidance Counselor Never Told You

The Secret Survival Manual

A Guidebook for Teens

✗✗✗✗✗✗✗✗✗✗✗✗✗✗✗✗✗✗✗✗✗✗✗✗✗✗✗✗✗✗

J. Brent Bill

✗✗✗✗✗✗✗✗✗✗✗✗✗✗✗✗✗✗✗✗✗✗✗✗✗✗✗✗✗✗

Illustrated by Rob Suggs

Fleming H. Revell
A Division of Baker Book House Co
Grand Rapids, Michigan 49516

Published by Fleming H. Revell
a division of Baker Book House Company
P.O. Box 6287, Grand Rapids, Michigan 49516-6287

Printed in the United States of America

Library of Congress Cataloging-in-Publication Data

Bill, J. Brent, 1951–
    The secret survival manual: a guidebook for teens / J. Brent Bill.
      p.   cm.
    ISBN 0-8007-5473-5
    1. Junior high school students—Religious life. 2. Junior high school students—Life skills. 3. Christian life—Juvenile literature. I. Title.
BV4531.2.B55   1993
248.8'3—dc20   93-14324

"Listen (Do You Want to Know A Secret)" on page 109 © 1964 John Lennon and Paul McCartney, Northern Songs Ltd. and Maclen Music, Inc.

To the kids in the New Castle First Friends Youth
Group for allowing Nancy and me to be a part
of their world

Acknowledgments
✗ ✗

In any great work of literature, the author alone is not responsible for whatever gems of wisdom or cleverly crafted phrases appear on the pages. The same is true even of "ungreat" works of literature, such as this one.

I have had a lot of help on this book (as with all my others). The seven kids who call Nancy and me mom and dad (as well as other things) have all contributed their parts to this book. Some are more visible than others, but each is valuable just the same. I know they don't think it's any big deal that I write, but for the inspiration (for both good and bad situations), I give them thanks. They are all good kids/adults, and all but one of them has survived junior high. And we have hopes that Tim will.

Nancy, my bride and best friend, is always a source of encouragement, understanding, and humor. She challenges me to write better and is always after me to write from the heart, not just the head. If I were writing about her, that would be easy indeed.

Finally, many thanks to the wonderful (or so they claim) kids at Parkview Junior High and the Seventh Grade Building in New Castle and Tri Junior High in Lewisville, Indiana. The kids at each school helped by writing down three questions they would most like answered. The questions in the book come from them. All are real questions by real kids and have not been corrected for grammar or speling, I mean spelling.

Their questions were interesting to read. Some of them were funny, some sad, some deep, some shallow. Each of them taught me a lot. Some reminded me of my days at Hilltonia Junior High, while others reminded me just how much the times have changed. Their questions are the heart of this book, so in many ways, it belongs to them.

Thanks, kids—and thanks also to your principals, Bob Crowe, Herb Bunch, and Mick Newport (all "Mister" to you)—for helping me out. I hope you each enjoy the book.

Most of all, I hope you buy one.

1

✗ ✗

How Do You Choose Your Friends?

There are many methods for choosing friends. I have heard a gallimaufry of them. Some of them were around when I was in school (back about 2200 B.C.), and some are brand-new. Maybe after going through this list, you'll find one or two you can use yourself.

The first method is what I call the "Yearbook Search." To use it effectively, you need your school's latest yearbook and a bright yellow highlighter.

Sit down with the yearbook open to the first page of the class you're going to be in. For example, if you are going to be an eighth-grader, look up all the eighth-graders. Then go on to the ninth-graders. You'll probably want to skip the seventh-graders, because who wants to hang around those *babies?*

Begin looking at the pictures and rating them on a scale of 1–10: 1 is socially unacceptable and 10 is your ideal friend.

This grading system awards points based upon how good-looking the people are. They get added points for being cheerleaders, involved in varsity sports, being rich, their parents' having a sports car, or any other such status sort of things. You decide what is important for your grading scale.

When you get to a person whose score totals 10 or more, highlight his or her picture with the marker and write down the score next to the name.

When you are done with your first pass through the yearbook, go back through it and list the twenty highest scorers. Then decide that they will be your friends.

Let them know of your decision. This can be done by phone, mail, or in person.

One problem with this method is that, once informed of your decision, they may not feel quite as honored as they should and decline your offer of friendship.

If they do this, just mark it up to lack of vision on their part.

The second method we'll cover is what's known as the "Mathletic Tryout." We've all heard of athletic tryouts—where you do your best so you can make the basketball or golf team.

The principle here is the same.

Say you're really bad at math.

"You're really bad at math."

Yes, I know I am (and I got the grades to prove it), but that's not what I meant when I said, "Say you're really bad at math." What I intended was for you to imagine that *you* don't do very well when it comes to mathematics.

You might have trouble with history or English, but math is the example we are going to use now. For one thing, "Mathlete" makes a better pun than "Histlete" or "Englete."

Let's pretend you can't handle quotients (to you, quotients are something a witch brews up in a kettle—you know, a magic quotient) and think a cosine is when your dad signed a loan with your big brother so he could get his first car. You are really bad at math.

How do you choose your friends?

The kind of friend you want to look for is a math-lete—someone who is as good in math as an athlete is in football or baseball. Because then you get a friend and good grades, too. A sort of three-for-one package. Ooops. I guess that's two-for-one. I told you I was bad at math. When you find a mathlete, you start hanging around him a lot, asking to see his homework, begging for help on yours, and generally hoping that some of his smarts will jump over onto you simply because you're around him.

One problem with this method is that the smarts won't jump over onto you just because you're hanging around a mathlete. It would be nice if they would, but they won't. Another problem is that trying to make a friend with someone just because it has some benefit (like higher grades) for you and none for him isn't a good way to make lasting friendships. If you want to find out how to make really good friends, keep reading.

The third method is the "Donald Trump Search." That's where you find a kid who has lots of money. Such a kid is usually easy to spot. Some clues are that he or she wears the latest fashions; arrives at school in a BMW, Mercedes-Benz, Volvo, or chauffeur-driven limousine; and has lunch catered into the cafeteria. She spends spring breaks at St. Croix and Christmases in the Caribbean.

You try to make friends with this person so you can spend Thanksgiving vacation in Vera Cruz or President's Day in Paris.

This method hardly ever works either.

That's one thing they all have in common—none of them works very well. And even when it looks as if they work, they don't.

For example, picking kids to be friends because of how they look has a major flaw. There are a lot of really good-looking people who are ugly on the inside. They have repellent personalities. They are like getting a really prettily wrapped gift that you open, only to find garbage.

Not a pleasant surprise.

Hanging around mathletes doesn't make you any smarter. Nothing of what they know rubs off just by being around them. Knowledge is not passed by osmosis or physical contact. You learn math (or any subject) only when you spend time studying it.

The Donald Trump Search doesn't pay off either. Somehow your "friends" catch on to the fact that you are hanging around them in hopes of free trips to Vail or Aspen. The few times you get invited over, you find you don't like them as much as you like the thought of being around all that money.

You end up being with the friends you already have.

I always did. I found that they chose me as often as I chose them. There wasn't a whole lot of effort to it. It really wasn't a conscious decision by either of us. We just found out that we liked the same things, laughed at the same stupid jokes, dressed the same way, lived in the same neighborhood, took the same classes, and played the same sports. What we had in common was our "sameness."

That's one of the best ways to choose friends. Search out people who are like you and whom you like.

That's not to say all your friends have to be the same. I have rich friends and poor friends. I have white friends and friends of color. I have male friends and female friends. I have found that each of them has something in common with me. They may not with one another, but they do with me.

So, a good way to choose friends is to find those people who share your interests. Then add some who will stretch your horizons.

There is someone who has already chosen you to be his friend. His interests are the same as yours but different too. He is always there for you to talk and share with but never forces you to be friends with him. He is available when you are ready to be friends.

His name is Jesus. His interests are like yours because his are unlimited. They are so big, they can include the same things you are interested in as well as things others are interested in.

He'll stretch your horizons because, just as his interests are unlimited, so is his power. He can take you places you've only imagined.

He's also a friend who will never leave or forsake you.

You'll want to have lots of friends. We all do. And choosing them is difficult. There is one choice that is easy if you want it to be. That's choosing to be a friend of Jesus. It will be the best choice of a friend you'll ever make.

2

XXXXXXXXXXXXXXXXXXXXXXXXXXX

Why Do Principals Wear Funny Clothes and Dorky Haircuts?

Because it's the law.

3

✗ ✗

How Do People My Age Get Headed in the Wrong Direction?

Getting headed in the wrong direction is easier than you may think—even for people who are smart. That's because life is a lot like a trip. In fact, life *is* a trip. It's a journey that lasts as long as we are alive and, as on any trip, it's important to have a good map.

When I was a teenager, our family took a trip from Ohio to California. We midwestern kids longed to see the surf, smell the salt-tinged air of the ocean, visit our grandparents, and most of all, go to Disneyland.

Our entire family (Dad, Mom, my three bratty little sisters, and I), along with our favorite uncle (Johnny), piled into another uncle's brand-new station wagon and headed west.

As a precaution against getting lost (which is pretty hard to do going to California from Ohio—all you have to do is point the car west and when you run into a large body of water that doesn't have any bridges across it, you know you've reached the Pacific Ocean and the California coast), Dad joined AAA and had them make out a Trip-tik.

In case you are wondering, a Trip-tik is a kind of flip open road map that has the trip broken down into short segments. It also warns of road construction, bridges that are out, and other things like that. Besides, it gave my bratty sisters something to do whenever they asked Dad how much farther we had to go.

This was a question that started about five blocks from home.

I had been a teenager for three years at that point, my first little sister had been one for one, and the next little sister was to be one soon. Dad was slowly losing all his patience with us as he realized he would be living with at least one teenager in his house for the next twelve years. If the first three he had endured were any indication, in his mind, happy years were not ahead.

As a result, Dad also learned to use the Trip-tik as a sort of semiguided missile toward the backseat, aiming at one of my sisters' heads (preferably the mouth) while growling, "See for yourself."

(After that, which was the last all-family trip, all of us kids learned to just shut up and ride in silence until we arrived at our destination—whether it was Grandma Bill's, two blocks away, or Florida, twenty hours away. I'm glad to say Dad is more patient now. Besides, I drive now and make *him* sit in the backseat and ask how far.)

At any rate, thanks to the Trip-tik (and a gag in Kathleen's mouth), we had no trouble making it to California.

We had taken a pretty direct route, and after about an eternity in the Pontiac, we arrived. We saw the surf, smelled the salt air, danced with Donald Duck at Disneyland, rode the rides at Knott's Berry Farm (I never did see any berries there), went to Tijuana, Mexico (where I bought firecrackers the size of small sticks of dynamite), and visited various relatives. It was a good time, and far too soon it was time to head home.

That's when trouble began.

Dad had AAA plan a scenic route for the return trip. It was Uncle Johnny's job to navigate this part of the journey, using the Trip-tik. For the most part, he did a fine job—except for one small error he made when we were in Utah. Uncle Johnny missed something on the map, and the next thing we knew we were deep in the wilds of Utah, about sixty miles in the wrong direction from where we should have been. We were lost in hostile wilderness.

Looking back on it, I guess it wasn't all hostile. We weren't surrounded by man-eating mountain lions or renegade cowpokes, or anything like that. As I recall, the only thing we were surrounded by were gas stations and an ice cream stand. Uncle Johnny bought us all whatever we wanted at that Dairy Queen. I suppose he did this to atone for his sin of getting us lost.

After finishing our ice cream, we slowly (and I do mean slowly, because we got caught in rain and road construction and didn't want to miss our turnoff *again)* made our way back the way we had come and finally found the right road home.

Due to losing time on our scenic trip through the wilds of Utah, Dad's carefully planned trip schedule was thrown off, and we lost our motel reservations at what was supposed to be our next stop.

That meant we had to drive from deepest, darkest Utah to Kansas City, Missouri, before we were able to find two vacant hotel rooms. That turned our ten-hour trip into a thirty-seven-and-a-half hour marathon through the heartland of America.

Trust me, there's not a lot to see in eastern Colorado and all of Kansas after the sun goes down—just miles and miles and miles of Interstate 70.

It was a lonnnggg trip.

Being the dutiful son I was, and since I had just gotten my driver's license, I did the only sensible, courteous thing a son could do. I curled up on the luggage in the back of the station wagon and slept for thirty-six-and-a-half hours of the thirty-seven-and-a-half hour trip.

Now to the moral of the story which is, we didn't get lost because we were a bad family. As a matter of fact, we're a pretty good family—even my bratty sisters, though I hate for them to know I feel that way.

We got lost because we couldn't read a map. We missed the signs that would have told us we were going the wrong way and that, instead of resting in the Rockies that evening, we were going to be navigating the prairie's highway across Colorado and Kansas in the moonlight for an eon.

Since life is a journey, the same can happen in life.

The reason some people your age get headed in the wrong direction is that many of them can't read maps. It's not because there aren't any maps. There are, if you just know where to find them.

One map is the life of another person. This map can be good or bad. Someone who has lived a good life can be an example of how to follow the best road. His or her life can be an example of the right way to go. If you live the way that person does, you'll find yourself on life's best roads.

Someone else can show you the wrong way to go— like where following the avenue of alcohol or the

19

street of selfishness or the highway of highs will take you. While it might be a scenic journey, the roads are rough and will tear up your vehicle (you) and wear it out before its time.

Either of these maps is good and serves a useful purpose. Each one can show you the way to go if you learn to read it right.

Another map is the Bible. It has lots of directions for going the right way. There are those who don't see it that way. They think of the Bible as a lot of don'ts—a list of stuff you shouldn't do. Some of it is, but that's not because God doesn't want you to have any fun. It's because it is a map showing you how to avoid bad roads in life.

The Bible has a lot of do's too. If you follow these do's, you'll find your life going a lot smoother. That's not to say the road the Bible shows is easy and smooth. Sometimes it even seems difficult.

At times, the smooth, easy way is the wrong way. It has become smooth and easy because of all the traffic traveling over it—you know, kind of like the grooves that develop in a freeway from all the trucks and cars going that way. It's easy to travel because you get stuck in the grooves. Grooves that are hard to get out of.

In these cases, the smooth way is the wrong way. You don't want to follow it just because it feels right.

That's why you need a map like the Bible, to help you make sure you are following the right road.

You can't control the maps other people use to direct their lives. As sad as it is, some of your friends will follow the wrong roads. They will get headed in the wrong direction. As a friend, you can try to point this out to them. You can tell them about the map you use and let them know that, as long as they are still on the journey, they can always turn around and head back toward the right road.

The most important thing you can do is make sure *you* keep going in the right direction. Use the maps life has given you. If you want to make sure you don't end up going the wrong way, look at the lives of people you think have it all together (no matter what their age), and continue checking the road map God gave you.

Bon voyage!

4

✗ ✗

Why Are There about Six Hours of School Monday through Friday?

Six hours of school? *Six hours of school!* You don't know how lucky you are. Most kids have to go to school about thirty hours Monday through Friday. If you are going to school just six hours Monday through Friday, you have a great schedule. Either that, or you are in a lot of trouble with the attendance office.

What's that? Oh, you meant why do you have to go to school six hours *every day* Monday through Friday, like every other kid. That throws a whole new light on your question. Six hours of school every day must seem like a terrible waste of time to you, and at times, it probably is.

That six hours could be put to really good use. You could sleep late, watch TV, go skateboarding, hit the mall, talk on the phone, or do any number of important teenager things. Instead, you're wasting your time in school. I agree there are some days spent in school that are a complete waste of time. That's not because it has to be. It's because you have made it that way. It's because you don't want to be there and have decided that putting in thirty hours or so a week at a stupid brick building is a terrible waste of your time. So you make it a terrible waste of time. You talk yourself into the idea that school is a bore and a waste, and so it is.

That's not why you are there. You are there that many hours a week for two main reasons—one of which (believe it or not) is not that your parents want you out of the house. These reasons are (1) your state legislature says you have to, and (2) it's really a good use of time.

Let's look at number one first (which is, after all, why it is number one—because it's first). The state legislature, in its wisdom, is responsible for setting all kinds of rules and regulations for how we get along in society. It makes rules for everybody and everything, from traffic regulations to how much "other food by-products" can go into hot dogs (which is something you'd rather not know). State legislatures have made lots of laws over the years—some of them good, some of them not so good, some helpful, and some that were probably helpful at one time but aren't any longer.

Concerning school hours, they made some good ones.

Part of the reason for spending thirty hours or so a week in school is that some folks (including me) think it's a good idea for you and your fellow junior-highers to spend at least as much time learning stuff as you do watching TV.

You may not realize it, but by the time the average teenager graduates, he or she will have spent more time watching TV than sitting in school. When you turn eighteen, you probably will have watched fif-teen-thousand hours of television. You'll have spent only eleven-thousand hours in school.

While watching TV may seem like a more attractive alternative to you, it shouldn't. It really isn't a very good use of time—especially compared with learning stuff at school.

"But," you say, "I learn a lot from television."

Sure you do. But is what you learn from television what you want to learn? Television teaches a lot about greed and murder and other anti-Christian stuff.

For example, did you know that you will see more than sixty-thousand murders during your lifetime of TV viewing? Some of them will be real, thanks to immediate, satellite coverage on the evening news.

You'll also watch over twenty-two-thousand commercials—mostly for stuff you don't need and which won't really make your clothes whiter, teeth brighter, or life better.

There's a whole lot more that TV teaches that you really don't need to learn, but that's a whole other book.

"Okay, okay," you say. "I won't stay home and watch TV. I'll listen to music or go to the movies instead."

Wrong. They can be just as bad as television, and when you stop and think about it, you know it's true.

So let's look at reason number two, which is, it really is a good use of time. That's the real reason the state legislature passed all those laws making you go to school.

"Why," you ask, "is going to school a good use of time?"

Because there is a lot to learn, and learning it is important if you want to do more than pump gas down at Lubner's Auto Lube for minimum wage. Unless that's what you want to do.

The world we live in is complex. You know that. What you may not realize is that it is going to get even more complex by the time you are an adult and out looking for a job.

When that time comes, you'll need every advantage you can get. Learning a bunch of stuff—no matter how worthless it may seem to you now—is one advantage you can have. But you'll have to go to school.

Lots of your friends, and maybe even you, think it's a waste to spend time learning English. You speak it every day. What else do you need to know? What else could you possibly learn about our language? Just spend a few minutes reading an owner's manual for a VCR or CD player, and you'll find out. Whoever wrote it should have spent more time studying English. If he or she had, you would be holding a manual you could understand and a VCR you wouldn't have to figure out by trial and error.

Let's look at math for a minute. What good will it ever do anyone? Did you know you'll use math almost every day? After you've placed your order at Wendy's you'll use math to make sure you received the correct change. At the end of your pay period you'll use it to double-check that your paycheck was the right amount (salary times hours worked) and that the correct percentage of taxes was withheld so that you don't end up owing Uncle Sam big bucks when you file your tax return. You may not even be aware you're using math, but the principles you've learned will help you in lots of situations. If you end up using a computer at work, as many people will, you'll discover that almost everything it does is based on mathematics.

We could do this for every subject—foreign language, gym, history, science—but you'd just get bored and think I was preaching at you. You'd be right. But, you've probably already got the point I'm trying to make.

Just in case you didn't, though, let me repeat it. The reason you're in school so much is that there's a lot to learn. I hate to tell you this, but you really don't know quite as much as you need to get by in this world.

Yes, there is a lot to learn about this world and the person who made it.

He's known as God. You probably already knew that, but how much do you really know about God? If you're like my kids (and me when I was their age), you probably think you know almost everything. God is love, Jesus is his Son, the Holy Spirit can live in us, the church is his people on earth, and the Bible was written under his direction. I know, why waste time in Sunday school and worship?

All of the above is true, but there's more. There's a lot to learn about God, and the only way you'll learn it is by spending a bit of your time in church or Sunday school.

What you will learn about God in those places will help you live a more fulfilling, challenging, and worthwhile life. What you learn will enrich you for the rest of your life.

There is more to life than spending time in class, but thirty hours at school and two or three hours at church every week is not too much to spend. Think of it as investing in your future and working to make it better.

Those hours you spend won't kill you. In fact, if you'll let them, they'll bring you life.

5

✗ ✗

Why Are There No More Recesses?

That's a question everyone who ever lived has asked. It's a question that goes as far back as the invention of junior high, which was in early Greece. But more about that in a later chapter. It's easy to see why this has been a universal question. Throughout your school career, recesses have been the highlight of the day. 'Til now.

Your elementary school schedule (at least from your point of view, if not from the teacher's) was built around recess, not the lessons. For six years (seven, if you went to kindergarten) you have known that school consisted of boring lessons, morning recess, more boring lessons, lunch, more boring lessons, afternoon recess, still more boring lessons, and dismissal. Even if it rained, you still had recess. You just had it indoors.

Now, when you've finally got school figured out, they change the rules. No longer is it a nice, tidy schedule of boring lessons, morning recess, more boring lessons, lunch, more boring lessons, afternoon recess, still more boring lessons, and dismissal. Nowadays it's home room, boring class, boring class, boring class, boring class, lunch, boring class, boring class, even more boring class, and dismissal.

What's wrong with this picture?

No recess!

Somebody left it out!

How could they do this?

Everyone knows that recess was a valuable part of your educational experience, as valuable as class time. Recess wasn't just a chance to go berserk and run around the playground and fall off the monkey bars and get sent to the nurses' office and have gravel picked out of your knees. No, it wasn't all fun. It was a learning time too.

One thing you learned was which kids would beat you up if you didn't let them win every game you played with them. Another thing was who was popular and who wasn't. That was pretty easy to learn. The popular kids were the ones who got chosen first for games, and the unpopular kids were the ones standing forlornly at the corner of the building, praying someone would ask them to play.

You also learned which part of the playground was out of the teacher's line of sight, so you wouldn't get caught doing something you shouldn't.

You learned the differences between boys and girls. Not anatomically. Socially. The main difference you learned was that boys always seem to get together and play games while girls like to get together and talk.

Now that's a generalization and, like all generalizations, it isn't completely true. There are lots of girls who like to play games and lots of guys who would just as soon stand around and talk. But most of the time, guys will huddle up around some kind of ball while the girls will huddle up around one another. Boys will try to knock each other on the ground and girls will talk each other into the ground. Sometimes the girls' talk is about the boys in the football huddle, since girls seem to be attracted to boys long before boys realize it's more fun to hold a girl's hand than a pigskin (though some girls' hands feel like pigskin).

Yes, recesses were valuable learning times. Now they've been taken away. What kind of stupid reasoning is there behind such a boneheaded move?

I've got bad, though probably not surprising, news for you. There isn't any. School is long on rules and short on reasoning—especially when it comes to things students seem to think are important. You know, things like longer breaks between classes, six weeks off for Christmas vacation, just one month of school each year, and recess.

Recess, as you have known it, is a thing of the past. What you have to do if you want to keep playing freeze tag with Tommy, Chris, Bruce, Scott, Evan, and Shaun or continue conversing with Edna, Tammy, Debbie, Linda, and Julie, is eat fast. Or nothing at all.

"What's eating got to do with recess?" you ask.

Everything.

That's because lunch should now replace recess as your favorite subject. If you are going to have anything in junior high that even closely resembles recess, it's going to have to take place during your lunch break. And we all know there's not much time there for wasting.

Here's some advice to help you make maximum use of your free time at lunch.

If you want to play, carry your lunch. Yes, it does seem kind of dorky, but you can grab your lunch out of your locker, wolf it down, and be outdoors on the athletic field before the first kid going through the cafeteria line has even arrived at the mashed potatoes.

If you want to carry on a conversation, go through the line with your friends. It moves slowly and you can chat over the chicken casserole, talk through the tomato soup, and gossip over the goulash. You get to eat and talk at the same time.

Both of these solutions, while not perfect, show what can be done if you use your time wisely and creatively.

Yes, recesses are a thing of the past. The funny thing is, soon you won't even miss them. It's part of growing up. You get tired of playing freeze tag and dodgeball or skipping rope and hanging upside down from the monkey bars. You'd rather do things like go to the sock hop in the gym on rainy days. Or watch a movie in the auditorium. It's all a part of growing up.

We all need time for recreation and relaxation. Recess just won't be that time anymore. God knew we needed time off. That's why there's a Sunday—a day of rest. In the Book of Genesis in the Bible is the story of how God created the world in just six days, with no recess—or even a lunch break.

You thought you had it tough.

After putting in those kind of hours, God knew some time off was needed. He came up with the Sabbath, a time to rest. Today we celebrate it on Sundays. It's meant to be a kind of recess or lunch break for our lives. Sundays are to be used for nourishment of our bodies and souls. They are to be times to get some spiritual food and soul rest. Times to break out of the routine of school and stuff and be re-created.

Spend some time this Sunday getting some spiritual food and playing. Make it your recess for life.

Well, there goes the bell. Lunch is over.

Let's get back to class.

6

✗ ✗

Why Do We Haf Two Teak Speling?

Eye dew knot no.

7

✗ ✗

Why Don't We Get Paid for Coming to School?

Good news—you do. I'm not kidding. You get paid for coming to school. Everybody does.

I don't mean you get a paycheck every Friday afternoon. Your principal doesn't hand checks out at the front door at 3:30 P.M. after you've left your locker and are heading for the bus or that long walk home. Nope, Mr. Vernables doesn't give you anything that looks like this:

O.C. Moore Memorial Junior High School
123 Jay Marshall Lane
Mullenville, Indiana 47366

Pay to the order of: Ima Goodstudent   475.00

The amount of: Four hundred seventy-five dollars and no cents
_____

                                        Teddy G. Vernables
                                        _____
                                        Teddy G. Vernables
                                        Principal

I know you wish he would. That would be nice. But if you are anything like the kids who have lived with Nancy and me, most of it would be spent before you got home at 4:00 P.M.

"But Dad, I really, really, really needed that CD—I mean the Dead Pet Shop Girls with Walk DMZ doing the 'Get Outta London Rap' is what everybody's listening to."

Or "Mommmmmmm! I couldn't live without that blouse. I mean the one I wore today is absolutely so out of date that I'll die if I wear it again. Besides, since we're the same size, you can borrow it whenever you want."

So even if you did get paid every Friday at the end of school, you probably wouldn't bank it toward your college education or any future major expenses.

No, new skateboards do not count as major future expenses.

The fact that you would spend the money as soon as you got it is not the reason you don't get a check every Friday.

"But," I can hear you saying, "I thought you said I got paid for going to school. How do I get paid if I don't receive money?"

You do receive money. Honest. It's just that its a deferred payment, which is a fancy way of saying you get it later instead of now.

"So how much later do I get it?" you ask.

When you start working.

"Wait just a minute," you sagely say. "How is that getting paid for going to school? That's money from my employer, not from going to school."

"Au contraire, mon frère" (which is French for "On the contrary, my friend"). You are receiving that money precisely because you did go to school. How long you stay in school will have a direct effect on the amount of money you take home each week from your job.

There are jobs out there that don't require a minimum of a high school education. There aren't many of them, but they are there. The only trouble is, they don't pay very much. If you were lucky enough to get a job as a waiter or waitress, you might make $3.85 or so an hour, plus tips. But not very long ago, the average American waiter made just $1.88 an hour. That's barely enough for a Big Mac, let alone Coke and fries.

There are lots of ads for nurses' aides, but if you stay in school and become a nurse instead of an aide, you'll make four times as much. Take that four times as much out over the life of your career, which will be at least thirty years, and you have a hefty chunk of change. Almost half a million dollars!

The more education you get, the more you get paid, generally.

That's not to say the only reason to stay in school is so you can make lots of money, but it is a nice side benefit. It's always nicer to drive the kind of car you want, live in a beautiful house, and go on vacation than it is to hope you find some extra money so you can pay the bills, avoid getting thrown out of the apartment, and watch other people's vacations on *"Vacations of the Rich and Famous."*

The real payoff of staying in school, though, is learning all you can so you will have a choice about what you are going to do with your life instead of having decisions forced on you. Because I stayed in school and even went to college, I have more options open to me than if I hadn't. A college degree opens doors that might otherwise be closed. The same is true of a high school diploma. Having one can make a lot of difference in helping you get to work where you want after graduating.

That might not seem important now, but it will when you are old—like around twenty-six or twenty-seven and want to get married or are married and want to have kids or are married, have kids, and they want to go on vacation and you have to say, "Sorry, kids, not this year or any year. I guess I should have stayed in school past the eighth grade, then perhaps I wouldn't be starting my twelfth year greasing cars for minimum wage at Lubner's Auto Lube."

That's not to say there's anything wrong with working for minimum wage or greasing cars for a living. If that's what you *want* to do. As long as it's a choice you make and not something you have to accept, especially when you could have done something about it earlier. Something as simple as staying in school.

There are nonmonetary ways you get paid for going to school as well. You learn stuff. You increase your career or college options. The more you learn, the more you discover possibilities for your future. You may end up taking a class that leads you in a direction you never thought of before. That happened to me with art class. I enjoyed it so much that I ended up studying it in college. Even though I don't use it daily today, art is something I still enjoy and do as a hobby. Okay, so that doesn't seem all that great right now. Trust me, someday you'll appreciate it.

Another payment is friends you make. These people pay off in your life—how they influence you and how they are there for you when you need them.

You also have the chance to participate in sports, clubs, drama productions, musical groups, and more.

These are all things that teenagers a hundred years ago didn't get to do. They got paid instead—but not for going to school—for putting in twelve-hour days at the shoe factory.

So, while you won't be bringing home a paycheck from school this week, you are banking one against your future.

If you are smart enough to check with God for directions from time to time, the payoff may be larger than you could ever imagine. He will always point you in the right direction.

8

✗ ✗

Why Are There Dress Codes?

That's a fair question. Why are there dress codes? It's not as if kids don't know how to put on clothes. Every teenager who ever lived was born with the innate good sense to dress correctly for the educational environment, right?

Well, maybe not. Not every kid dresses right for school. But you are not every kid. You and your friends are covered correctly, aren't you?

Since you already know how to dress, it might help you to think of the dress code as a guideline (heavily enforced) for the goofballs who don't. You know the ones I mean—the kids who are wearing short shorts in the middle of winter; midriff T-shirts advertising beer, tobacco, or dirty jokes; skirts so short you can see their armpits or jeans so tight you can see. . . . um, well, you get the idea. These kids are the reason for having a dress code.

Some people can dress awfully funny. Both funny as in "ha ha" and as in *strange*. And funny dressers can be distracting.

It's awfully difficult to pay attention to *history* when the girl the next seat over is wearing a dress packed tightly with *her story*. Giving attention to geography is almost impossible when all you're getting is a glimpse of the canyon created by the too-short T-shirt and too-small pants on the guy in front of you.

Face facts. There are a lot of people out there who don't know how to dress for school. What may work for a Dead Pet Shop Girls concert or an outing at the mall, doesn't necessarily go for school.

You're okay. As we decided earlier, you know the difference. The rules are there to help those poor unfortunate children who don't. They are regulations set up by the Fashion Police. After all, everyone needs to learn something at school. Maybe these clothing criminals will finally learn how to dress.

Dress codes aren't anything new. The first one is mentioned in the Bible. It came from the ultimate code maker—God. God came up with the first one in the Garden of Eden.

It turned out he didn't much care for the fig leaf fashions Adam and Eve had developed on their own, so he instructed them in the fine art of sartorial splendor for living in the outside world. Check out Genesis if you want to see what they wore. It sure wasn't Guess? or Calvin Klein.

You see, up to that point, clothes weren't necessary. Nudity was natural, so it was not distracting. Everything was good, and Adam didn't giggle when Eve walked into the Garden naked. Well, maybe he did, but not for the same reason a lot of kids laugh at anything sexual. He had a good and natural giggle.

Then came sin. And what was clean somehow felt dirty. Some of that dirt has rubbed off on all of us. Dress codes are one of the results. We need to learn how to dress appropriately for the situation. We can dress to excite or draw attention to ourselves or to just plain look good.

Dress codes may not seem like much fun, but they do serve a purpose. They help us focus on why we are in school instead of who's sitting next to us or what beer is sponsoring what rock group's latest tour.

All in all, a dress code is for everybody's good. It keeps you from being distracted from the task at hand and teaches tacky dressers how to dress right whether they want to or not.

Now, go shine your shoes and iron that blouse. As daughter Laura says, "It is important to look good."

God adds, "Inside and out!"

9

✗ ✗

How Long Are
the Longest Fingernails?

The *Guinness Book of World Records* says that Shridhar Chillal of Poona, India, has a thumbnail of 27½ inches and that the total length of the fingernails on his left hand equals 108½ inches.

10

✗ ✗

How Come We Can't Pick Our Own Teachers?

Because, given a list like this:
☐ A. Mr. Fischvogt
☐ B. Mrs. Banker
☐ C. Ms. Hannon

Most of you would pick:
☐ D. None of the above

You know that's true. Most of the time, you feel that no teacher is better than some teacher. But for the sake of argument, let's say you chose Ms. Hannon. What are your reasons behind such a choice? Are they good ones? Or is it because she's pretty? Or because she's known to grade on a curve? Or because no one has ever failed her class? Or because she's dating your older brother and you figure that's worth at least a B+?

Chances are it's not because you've heard she's the smartest teacher there. Or that getting an A in her class is going to require some real effort. Or that she assigns lots of homework and expects it all done—neatly and on time.

No, left to your own devices, you would probably choose teachers for the wrong reasons.

"He's cute."

"She doesn't take attendance."

"My older sister had him and got really bad grades, so I ought to look good compared with Madilyn."

Those are all reasons, but they aren't valid ones. That's why the school doesn't let you pick your teachers. It's not because you're exceptionally incompetent or different from any other teenager who has ever lived. Through the ages, school administrators have known that, given a chance, kids would pick teachers for the wrong reasons. They might seem right at the time, but they'd be wrong in the long run.

Say you picked Ms. Hannon because she's pretty. So what? Do you think you're going to be dating her? You're in her class forty-five minutes a day, five days a week. Come Friday night, she's not thinking of you. Her mind's on Kelly Daugherty, that new salesman who just sold the school a photocopy machine. You're not even history to her. On Friday night, as she gets ready for her date, you're *pre-history*, something unrecorded in her memory's data bank.

Okay, so you signed up because she grades on a curve. All that means is you don't have to try very hard, and you spend a lot of time praying that nobody else does either. If everybody else is like you, you'll be okay—at least as far as grades are concerned. But if one kid blows it, actually does something stupid like studying hard and getting a 100 percent on her tests, suddenly your 75 has turned into a C- instead of a B+.

So much for teachers with curves.

Well, at least no one has ever failed one of her classes. That sounds like a good reason, but even it has a major flaw. If it's so easy no one has ever failed, chances are no one's learned anything either. If it's such a breeze, why bother sitting through it? Why would you want to waste forty-five minutes a day, five days a week, not learning anything? You've got to put in the time, so why not make it count for something? You could at least learn something while you're stuck there.

Finally, she's dating your older brother. Well, she *was.* That was when the semester started. Now she's going out with Mr. Daugherty. She dumped your brother because she thinks he's a jerk. So what does that make you? Why, a younger jerk, of course. And even though she's used your brother's picture for a target on her dart board so much that it could now be used as a window screen, she still has a lot of pent-up anger. Your brother's not around to take it out on. But you are. What does *that* do to your grade?

You should have thought of that earlier.

So even though your reasons might have looked good at the start, in the long run they may work against you—and in junior high, you want everything you can working for you.

While the school may not let you pick your teachers you do get to choose some teachers. That's when you are picking the people who are going to help you learn the important things of life—stuff like sex, drugs, morals, and so on. You have a lot of say about who will help you in those areas.

Choosing wisely in these subjects might be even harder than choosing the right teacher for eighth-grade math. That's because there are lots of choices. Many of them are urging you to pick them. Who are you going to choose—your friends, parents, older siblings, the church? Are you going to use all of them? Or none?

Yes, it's a tough decision. You want, no, you need, to make the right one. At school, all you are risking is a grade and some time not learning anything. With these other choices, you are risking your life.

How do you know the right teachers to pick? Well, it's a cinch that the most attractive or easy way isn't the best. You learned that earlier when we talked about picking teachers for classes. In picking teachers for life, you need to choose those who have lived well and who know the right answers to the subjects you want to learn.

Look for those folks whom you respect, not necessarily those you like or think are fabulous, but people you feel have put the stuff of life together and are living the way they should.

Check out the church and see if it teaches what the Bible says.

Always ask why of those who would teach you. Schoolteachers may not always like you asking that, but in life, if people are confident in their answers, they won't be afraid to tell you why.

So ask your pastor why he believes what he does. Do the same of your friends. And parents. And other would-be teachers.

Finally, talk to the ultimate teacher—Jesus. He's got some great answers, is a good Teacher, and is never afraid of the question *why*? You can ask him anything. Anytime. About anything. Just listen carefully and quietly for his answer. If you do, you will learn more than you can imagine.

Choose your teachers wisely, and always ask for the ultimate teacher—Jesus.

11

XXXXXXXXXXXXXXXXXXXXXXXXXX

Why Do Some People
Think Everything Is a Joke?

Do you know why cannibals never eat clowns?

Excuse me, I guess that's not a very good way to begin answering this question. If I continued with that joke, you might think I wasn't taking you seriously and I was one of those people who thinks everything is a joke.

That's not to say I've never been accused of that. At times I don't seem to take things seriously, I guess. I think most people get told that at one time or another. That's most likely because many of us tend to say things we think are funny and nobody else does, or we laugh out loud at the wrong time—like at a funeral or in church (during the serious part). Sometimes we are just trying to lighten the mood, and other times we think of something funny and can't help ourselves. So we get charged with being people who don't take anything seriously and have to laugh at everything. But it's not true. We don't have to laugh at everything. We don't think everything is a joke. No one does. There is no one on this earth who thinks everything is a joke.

Some people act as if they do, though. They want you to think nothing bothers them and they find everything funny. They want you to believe they think it's a hoot to flunk algebra, break up with a boyfriend, or get suspended.

This kind of person makes fun of everything and everyone, including you—even when you are his or her best friend. He prides himself on being the class clown or she the funny girl who can get a laugh anytime, anywhere, at anyone's expense.

Humor is important. We all want to have fun and laugh and have a good time. That's true for all of us.

It's also important to know when enough is enough. Some people don't seem to know when that point has been reached, or maybe they do but they just keep going. Why? Maybe because they are hiding.

Humor is a great concealer, a lot like the big tree in the backyard that you used to hide behind while playing Hide-and-Seek. You could peek out from around it and see what was going on, but so long as you stayed right behind it, no one could see you. Treating everything as a joke is the same thing. It makes the real you almost invisible.

You see, if you treat everything as a big joke, then nobody takes you too seriously, and you don't have to take life too seriously—at least on the surface.

That's what I mean by hiding. Some kids (and adults) cover up their real feelings by joking all the time. If you are always telling a joke or making fun of something, nobody can tell how much stuff is really bothering you. You can hide your feelings. It lets you keep others at a distance that you consider safe.

Yes, humor makes a great wall that hides what's behind it—what's inside you. Some people use humor as a way to try to keep hurt on the outside. At least they keep others on the outside, so they can't see the pain. But pain is part of life. Everybody hurts and everybody has sorrow in their lives. Some folks live with, accept, and conquer it. Other people don't know how to handle it, so they cover it with humor.

Instead of getting mad at people who seem to treat everything as a big joke, maybe you could spend some time trying to understand them. Let them know you care about their feelings. All of them—whether happy or sad.

If you can do that, you might be able to help a "joker" begin tearing down the wall he or she has built, joke by joke, until you can see the real person living behind it. You can help him learn when humor is right and necessary and one of the best parts of life.

God wants us to enjoy life. God has a sense of humor. Why else do we have animals that look like the aardvark or bald guys like your dad and me?

Enjoy the humor in life. Help others do the same. Then work with them so they can see that it's okay that life isn't one big joke after another. It's okay to cry, even. Jesus did. We can too. Someday we may look back on what we cried about and laugh.

Oh, by the way, the reason cannibals don't eat clowns is—they taste funny.

12

✗ ✗

Why Do You Always Make Stupid Mistakes on Tests?

One reason is that there is no such thing as a smart mistake. Any mistake you make on a test is a stupid one. It's stupid because you look at it later and say, "Man, was that dumb."

So, you will always make stupid mistakes on tests.

If the question is why do you make mistakes on tests, then the answers are not so obvious. They are obvious but not as obvious as "stupid mistakes."

There are lots of reasons a person makes mistakes on tests. One heard frequently is, "I forgot to study."

This happens all the time at our house. "I forgot I had a test today." Why is it easy to remember what time next week the MTV program you want to record comes on and how to set the VCR to pick it up at 3:00 A.M. PST, but you can't remember you have a final exam tomorrow?

It's not as if one-third of your grade is riding on it or anything. So you get busy listening to CDs or playing basketball or talking on the phone. Then the next day, you walk into Mrs. Sawicki's room and whammo, the light goes on. "We're having a test today. I should have studied!" You didn't. You make mistakes. You would have been smart to study. You blew it—that's a stupid mistake.

Another reason is that you get nervous. Mr. Rugh hands out tests, and your mind turns to Jell-O. Every-

thing you have ever learned about any subject gets sucked out of your brain by a mysterious vacuum that operates only when the words *test, pop quiz* (which is not a quiz about Pepsi, Coke, or your dad), and *final exam* enter the eyeballs.

Still another reason is you just don't pay close enough attention to the test paper itself. You get like a person on "Family Feud" who buzzes in before the question is out of the host's mouth. You read a part of the question and answer it, and when you get the test back you find out you should have read the whole thing because you missed the most important part of the question—the part that counted the most toward your grade.

For example, you read "What year did Columbus . . ." and you answer "1492" because you know that's the year he sailed "the ocean blue" and "discovered" America (which was a great surprise to the people who were already living here and didn't know they hadn't been discovered yet and after they were, wished they hadn't been).

You get the test back two days later and find out that "1492" is wrong, not because that's not when Columbus thought he had made it to India (which he hadn't—he was in reality closer to Indian-a) but because the question was, "What year did Columbus, Ohio, native James Thurber write "The Night the Dam Broke?" So you made a stupid mistake.

Actually, you made two. One was not reading the question correctly. The second was thinking you were in history class when you were really in English class.

Not paying attention is the main reason for lots of stupid mistakes—on the tests life hands out as well as the ones in school.

Sometimes we don't study, so we're not prepared. Most of the time we just don't pay attention to what's happening. We get mixed up with the wrong group of kids, and the next thing we know, we're shoplifting something from K-Mart because everyone else we're with is doing it. We don't want our friends making fun of us. Then we wind up sitting down at the police station trying to figure out what we're going to say to Mom and Dad when they come to pick us up.

If they come to pick us up, we think to ourselves.

One way to avoid making stupid mistakes on life's tests is to listen to the voice inside. God has put his spirit in each of us to guide us. But God speaks very quietly. That voice doesn't come across a PA system. Our internal volume control is not set on 10. It's more like 1. God does speak clearly—just softly.

We need to slow down and learn to listen for that voice. If we do, we avoid lots of stupid mistakes.

Even if we do make mistakes, and we all do, they become stupid only when we refuse to learn from them. Every mistake contains a lesson, no matter how painful. Decide to learn something from it and go on wiser because of it.

Or don't learn, and just go on—still stupid.

If you want to avoid stupid mistakes—pay attention. In school, read the whole question. In life, listen to God's voice inside. And if you do mess up, learn something. Like not to do something that stupid again!

13

XXXXXXXXXXXXXXXXXXXXXXXXXX

Why Do Teachers Have Pets?

Teachers have pets for the same reason you do. That is, they like and want the companionship a pet provides. This is something they need. Everyone knows teachers don't have any friends. How could they—they're teachers! Who would want to hang around with them?

Their only alternative to human fellowship is to have a dog, cat, hamster, or goldfish to come home to after a long, hard day of being nasty to junior high kids. Nothing warms the cockles (whatever they are) of a teacher's heart (as if they had them) like a cocker spaniel's warm, wet greeting after the last bell has rung.

What's that? Oh, that's not the kind of pet you meant. You were referring to that kid (or those kids) the teacher seems to like more than all the others. You meant the kid who gets to pass out the test papers, gets all A's, and answers all the easy questions. You meant THE FAVORITE.

That's a whole other question—one that requires a lot of thought.

There, I'm through thinking about it.

My answer is—I'm not sure. I have a sneaky suspicion that it's for the same reason you have favorite friends.

My reason for that is, and again I'm not sure, I think teachers are human—at least some of the ones I know are. It may be that most of them are. As such, they have all the human emotions you and I have. Well, a lot of them anyway.

That means they have kids in their classes they are inclined to like more than others. Therefore, these teachers tend to talk to them more and treat them nicer than the other kids. These kids then become known as "teachers' pets."

The kids teachers pick to be pets probably aren't really to blame themselves. All they did was show up for class with their homework neatly done and assignments completely read, act interested in what the teacher was saying, and study hard for tests.

Okay, so maybe it is their fault. No normal kid would do something nefarious like that. It's just not a part of the accepted teenage code of ethics.

In spite of that abnormal behavior, teachers really shouldn't play favorites, should they? They ought to know better. They are adults, after all. It isn't fair.

Unfortunately, life isn't fair, and neither are all teachers, so some of them play favorites.

Being in a class where there's an obvious pet is no fun, especially for those who aren't the pet. And they know they aren't. It is easy to feel discriminated against. They feel they don't have a chance compared with the pet.

Being the teacher's pet isn't always a picnic either. I know that's difficult to believe, but think about it. If you are the teacher's pet, there is only one person in the room who likes you. That's the teacher.

The other kids don't. Why should they, when you've got everything going for you? That's how the other kids feel, whether it's true or not. You may be receiving more attention, but the teacher isn't cutting you any slack. He or she might even be expecting more from you because you are the favorite. The teacher depends on you to get better grades and work harder because she sees your potential, and the kids hate you for having it so easy.

Being a teacher's pet is often a lousy position to hold. Fortunately, most teachers are pretty good about not having pets. There are times you think one of your classmates is a pet because you feel he or she is treated better than you are—which may not be true. If it is true, it's usually for the reasons I stated before—that person has done the homework, studied hard, and other stupid stuff like that.

If you haven't done all those things, and Mrs. Faris responds to the kid who has, you feel as though she's playing favorites. That makes you feel cruddy and less than a favorite—a sort of academic also-ran.

It's too bad for everyone that some teachers have pets. It hurts both those who aren't the pet and the kid who is.

Now for some good news. You are one teacher's pet. You really are. You are a pet of the best teacher of all. His name is Jesus. Jesus was a pretty good teacher when he was on earth. People used to flock to hear him teach. He excelled at teaching in all kinds of groups. He taught teachers, preachers, priests, fishermen, and tax collectors. He taught in small groups. He taught in large ones. Why, one time he had a student/teacher ratio of 5,000 to 1.

The unique thing about Jesus was that everyone was his pet. He treated everybody as equals. He expected everyone to do the best they could according to their abilities—and then helped them do it.

The Bible tells us Jesus is the same forever. The way he was yesterday is the way he is today and will be in the future. That's really good news.

It means you are now, and always will be, Jesus' pet—his favorite. That's because he loves you as much as he loves everybody. He wants the best for you and will do what he can to make sure you get A's in all of life's lessons.

While it may bother you that Mrs. Huston has her favorite, remember that you're somebody's favorite too. If you should have just one teacher who likes you, isn't it better to have the Master Teacher like you than the math teacher?

You know it is, even when semester grades come out.

14

✗ ✗

Why Can't We Have Four Months Off for Summer Vacation?

Because studies done by the National Educational Research Department of Studies (N.E.R.D.S.) have shown that in a three-and-a-half-month period, a young person between the ages of thirteen and eighteen forgets everything learned during the previous eight-and-one-half months.

School boards are not going to take any chances that you will have to be taught things over again. They don't want you in school any longer than you want to be there.

15

✗✗✗✗✗✗✗✗✗✗✗✗✗✗✗✗✗✗✗✗✗✗✗✗✗✗

Where Does the Cafeteria Get Its Food?

It is from dungeons dark and grimy,
from pits both bottomless and slimy,
they bring forth these incredible
concoctions, which are supposedly edible.
Yet, if so, what is the taste in your mouth?
Would they mind if you spit it out?
For, as it off your tray crawls:
your voice, it outwardly calls
to kill it, to stop it,
but never never ever eat it!
"What is this mess?" you silently ask,
waiting for a response from those who stroll past.
"Why, my son," the principal cooed,
"eat it up; it's cafeteria food!"

—Benjamin Bill

This is one of the mysteries of the ages. Just where does the cafeteria get that stuff they claim is food? Of course, another question is, why, if everybody hates this bilge so much, do they stand in line to eat it and then come back for seconds? But that's another question for another portion of this book. Back to the original question—where do they get that *food?*

If you have been keeping up with your social studies, you'll remember studying environmental issues. Among the most pressing of these issues today are those of solid waste landfills and toxic waste disposal.

"Solid waste landfills" is simply a nice way of saying what everyone else knows is really a dump. No, not your bedroom, the place the garbage trucks take your trash bags after you fill them with all sorts of unsavory edible and inedible remains.

Dumps, excuse me, landfills are filling up faster than expected. Some states have run out of landfill space and are trucking their trash across state lines or putting it on barges and sinking it in the ocean.

Some states, particularly the ones being dumped in (and on), and a lot of whales, are taking a dim look at these two practices and don't want other people "dumping your trash in my backyard" (or swimming pool, in the case of the whales).

That's nontoxic waste—stuff that is smelly and kind of gross-looking but basically not harmful. Just unpleasant.

Then there's the toxic stuff. Poison stuff. Stuff that will peel all your skin off or kill all your brain cells if you even look at it. Nobody wants that stuff. Well, almost nobody.

Thank heaven for the schools of America. Everybody knows teenagers will eat anything—and everything. I just finished watching one of our children, Ben, eat what he called a sandwich. He made it on an egg bun, added two slices of dried beef, smothered that with horseradish sauce and green onion potato chip dip, and topped the whole mess off with sliced olives.

I think that proves my point.

Schools know kids will eat anything. They also know they have to feed you something. What it has to be is cheap. I don't mean affordable for you. I mean cheap for them. They can charge you anything they want, but they have to make money on the meals so they can pay the people they call cooks.

Since cheapness is the essence of school lunches, the first place they go is to the government. The schools buy up all the surplus cheese, milk, other dairy products, peanut butter, and canned goods they can. This helps the government get rid of all this stuff that is filling up warehouses around the country, which means the government has room again to buy even more surplus cheese, milk, other dairy products, peanut butter, and canned goods.

All that surplus food is still not enough. Many of you are cavernous carnivores—virtual bottomless bellies.

So they contact the local department of sanitation and offer to provide a place for it to store solid and toxic waste. Your tummy.

After all, you're a teenager. You'll eat anything.

Just to make sure it won't do you too much harm, they cram it full of vitamins A, B_{1-6}, C, D, and X, Y, Z_{inc}. That way they feed you cheap, get your stomachs full, make sure you get the minimum daily allowance of vitamins and minerals, and solve a pressing environmental issue all at the same time.

Now you know one of the best-kept secrets of modern time—where they get the food they feed you in the cafeteria. It's a combination of government leftovers (and you thought Mom's were bad), garbage, and crowded-in vitamins.

Well, that's not really where they get it. Not all of it anyhow. But the FBI (the Food Buyers Industry) made me promise not to tell the whole story.

Regardless of where they get it, you eat it. The side effects are not too bad or permanent. They consist mainly of short-term memory loss when it comes test time and urges to sleep through boring classes.

There is good food to be had in this world, though it isn't found in the cafeteria or in any kitchen. It's the Bread of Life. That's another name for Jesus. The Christian faith tells us that if we partake of him, that is, feed on his life and sacrifice for us, we will have a meal that will satisfy our very souls.

I know that sounds a little strange—feeding on Jesus. But it doesn't mean literal cannibalism. It means living so close to him that doing so nourishes our souls and helps us grow—the same way good food works on our bodies.

The next time you're eating baffling bread (it's baffling because you can't figure out what's in it) in the school cafeteria, chock-full of all those healthy vitamins, think of the vitamin you really need—vitamin J. Vitamin Jesus.

How do you get Vitamin J? Why, just in *vit him in.*

16

✗ ✗

Who Dreams Up the School Menu, and Why Do They Make Us Eat It?

This question goes with the last one. That's because it too has to do with cafeteria food. (I thought I'd better explain that to you in case you wondered what the two had in common.)

The school menu development process is largely shrouded in secrecy, much like the making of hydrogen bombs was in the 1950s and 1960s. Everyone knew they existed and was scared to death of them but didn't really know how they got made or who to blame for them.

Now, at long last, the truth can be told.

No, not about H-bombs—about the school menu.

If you read my answer to the last question (which is a bold assumption on my part, I know), you now know where the ingredients for school lunches come from. What you don't know is who puts them together in the combinations you find in the cafeteria—and why you have to eat them.

You probably think your principal and teachers have something to do with it. They don't.

The truth is, three people make up the menu. For years, they have served secretly on a committee whose makeup was known to only two people in America. One was the President of the United States. The other wasn't. Finally, after minutes of intense investigation, I have uncovered the heretofore secret identities of the people who control the school lunch menu. They are the custodian, the boss of the bus drivers, and the head of the home economics department.

These three meet at the beginning of each year and develop a plan for feeding you for two entire semesters. Each person has his or her own unique reason for being on the committee. Each has a task to perform, a strategy to put into place.

Mr. Brooks, the custodian, is intent on designing a menu that has a modicum of cleaning up associated with it. In other words, he wants food that will flush off the floor, wash off the walls, and come off the ceiling easily. He doesn't care if it tastes good or is nutritious, so long as it comes off the building with a minimum of soap, water, and work.

Mr. Paporello, *cappo di drivers di busos* (which is sort of Italian for "chief of all the bus drivers"), wants a menu that won't be coming up on the bus floor on the way home. The buses are hard enough to clean up at the end of the day without having to hose out heaved hash from today's luncheon special. He prefers food that stays together in slimy pools or large chunks that are easily swept into piles.

Finally, there's Mrs. Millikan, queen of the home ec department. Her word is law. Her goal is to come up with a menu that makes even the stuff the seventh-grade home ekkies create look good. This is hard to do. You've seen some of the seventh-grade home ec cooking projects. Carrie, Meagan, Melissa, Cindy, and Shannon bake brownies that could pass a building inspector's scrutiny and be used in constructing the new addition to the gym. Jesus was tempted by Satan

Who dreams up the school menu and why do they make us eat it?

to turn stones into bread. In junior high home ec, without any temptation from the devil at all, the students turn bread into stones. All the time.

It is these three—Brooks, Paporello, and Millikan—who conspire over consumables. They plan and plot the provisions you will pour down your gullet. They are the ones who envisage the school menu.

Now, why do they make you eat it? They don't. You do that all on your own. Which is something that has even Brooks, Paporello, and Millikan mystified. They wouldn't. They don't. They bring their lunches in brown bags and eat in the staff lounge.

But you eat it, because for some strange reason you think it's food. No one holds a gun on you and makes you do it. No guards force you to go through the line, your tray held in front of you, accepting whatever is slapped down on it. You and your friends willingly line up, pay your money to that curmudgeonly cafeteria worker, and eat the stuff. Then you try to blame someone else for making you do so.

That happens in life sometimes too. We like to place the blame on others for stuff we have chosen to do. Most of the time, though, we are the only ones to blame.

Just as no one forces you to eat the mystery meals, no one forces you to cheat, lie, steal, or do anything else as distasteful to your soul as the cafeteria food is to your stomach.

There used to be a character on TV named Geraldine. Geraldine excused everything she did by saying, "The devil made me do it." That wasn't true for her—and it isn't true for you either. It is up to you, and you alone, to decide which of the choices that life's cafeteria has to offer you'll put on your tray.

There are people planning life menus. Some of them are good, some are bad, and some are deadly. Ultimately, all these planners are doing is writing their menus on the board. You are the one responsible for making the selection. Take your time. Study the menus. Ask whether what is on them is stuff you really want to make a part of your life.

It's okay to ask for help too. You should seek advice from folks who have been through the line before you, made their selections, and didn't end up with heartburn of the soul.

You can also ask God for help. He knows all the choices that have been put on the menu boards. He knows what's good for your soul and what will give you indigestion.

Make your choices wise ones. With God's help, they will be.

17

✗ ✗

Why Do They Keep Serving Bad Food?

I don't think you've been paying very close attention. They keep serving bad food because you keep eating it.

Think about this for a minute. If you didn't eat the stuff, they'd quit serving it.

That's not to say they'd quit making it, but they wouldn't serve it to you because if you didn't go through the lunch line, there wouldn't be anyone to serve it to.

So you see, in the end, bad school food is nobody's fault but your own.

If you don't want bad food, just quit eating.

18

XXXXXXXXXXXXXXXXXXXXXXXXXX

Why Do I Hate Art?

This is a very difficult question. What makes it so hard is I'm not sure which Art you're speaking of. I only know one Art, and he's a pretty nice guy, so I'm pretty sure he can't be the one you hate.

Maybe you could send me more information, and then I could answer your question better.

19

xxxxxxxxxxxxxxxxxxxxxxxxxxx

Why Do Teachers Talk So Much?

Teachers who talk in class are real nuisances. You would think they would be more considerate and just let you learn in peace and quiet. All that racket they make by talking and talking and talking disturbs your concentration. How are you supposed to learn if they keep distracting you?

It's not as if their talking is all that important or necessary. It doesn't add anything to your ability to learn. You can learn without their verbalizing. You've got books, reading assignments, pens, paper, and loads of homework. Why do they have to talk?

Surely they can trust you to learn the material. You already take your time and memorize each and every paper they hand out and every book that is assigned, don't you? Of course you do.

And they have to go and ruin it all by talking.

Okay, maybe I am being a little sarcastic about the whole thing. But let's think about this for a minute. How is a teacher supposed to teach without speaking— unless, of course, you are attending mime school? In that case, the teacher had better *not* talk.

There are some ways a teacher could do it, I guess. She could draw pictures on the board, then have you guess what the drawing is about—a sort of educational Win, Lose or Draw or Pictionary. The scientific theory of photosynthesis might be kind of hard to figure out from pictures on a blackboard, though.

Or there's the Charades method. That's the one where the teacher acts out the lesson, divides the class into teams, and times responses to his role plays. Once again, this might be really tough in some subjects. It's hard to act out a long-division problem.

There are other ways of teaching without talking. Mr. Sitler, your history teacher, could try to communicate the way you and your friends do. Kids have discovered lots of nonverbal ways to communicate, haven't they? One is through body language. The way you sit or stand or shrug or give eye contact indicates interest in a subject—or lack of it. The way you look at people can tell them volumes, more than words could, even. A simple glance can say, "I really like you" or "I wish you would drop dead."

Body language usually works best for communicating feelings, though, not history dates. So maybe it wouldn't work very well in school after all.

How about note passing? That might work better. Your social studies teacher could just write down the important points of the lesson, fold it up into a really, really, really small square, and pass it to a kid in class.

Note passing works for kids because you're getting notes from people you want to hear from. Your friends are writing stuff you want to read—stuff like who's going with whom, or in trouble with her parents, or getting kicked off the basketball team. Chances are you don't want to read a note about Japanese diplomats Saburo Kurusu and Kichisaburo Nomura's mission to the United States State Department on December 7, 1941. You should, but you probably don't.

So, even though these techniques might work fine for you and your friends, it is unlikely that they would be effective in any kind of educational setting. It's terribly hard to communicate algebra with a shrug (although I always shrugged whenever I thought about algebra). It's no easier to teach art by passing notes.

Even you and your friends find you have to talk sometimes. The only reason you communicate nonverbally is that you'll get in trouble talking out loud in class or study hall. Nonverbal communication is second choice. There are times that talking is the only way to express what needs to be communicated. You just have to say it.

It is the same for teachers. They have to talk about the material they are trying to get across to you, if you are ever going to understand it. It may be annoying (and interrupting your sleep), but it's the only way.

Teachers are not the only ones who talk all the time in an attempt to teach. Parents (another especially troublesome group to many of you) do too. Talking to teach is an annoying adult trait.

God talks to us all the time too. He does. God is speaking to us constantly. He uses some intriguing ways. For example, at times he speaks through people. He talks to us through our friends, our pastors, our teachers—and even our parents. We may not recognize it as "God talk," but it is.

God also talks to us through nature. Its beauty and order can tell us a lot about how we should live.

Most of all, God speaks through, and to, our souls—if we will get quiet and listen.

That's the unique thing about the way God talks. He speaks very quietly, whether it's through people, nature, or our souls. We have to be very still if we want to hear God talk. It's the only way we will recognize it as "God talk." But if we do, we will learn many things.

So, the next time Mr. Finster is droning on and on about Neil Armstrong's "giant step," think about what you might be learning if you just tune in to what's being said—both by him and by God.

20

✗✗✗✗✗✗✗✗✗✗✗✗✗✗✗✗✗✗✗✗✗✗✗✗✗✗✗

How Many Animals Are There in the World?

4,593,972,001,436.5 (not including flies)

21

XXXXXXXXXXXXXXXXXXXXXXXXXXX

Why Do Kids Have to Put Down Other Kids So Much —Like about Where They Live and What They Look Like and Stuff?

That's a question people have been trying to answer for centuries. Why do people make fun of, or put down, other people? It's hurtful. It's mean. It's hateful. If it's all those things, why do people do it?

One reason could be that it's one way to help them not feel so bad about who they are. When Rufus is not feeling too good about himself, he thinks he might feel better if he focuses everyone's attention on someone else. He might feel kind of inadequate. He wants to be a better person than he is. So, when somebody else messes up, he makes fun of him or her or draws attention to the misstep. That way he can feel superior to the person in trouble.

Or maybe Carla, who is overweight, is really self-conscious about being so heavy. To divert attention from herself, she makes fun of the kid who's extra skinny. While it's not very nice, Rufus and Carla feel better about themselves because they put others down. Focusing on another's misfortune allows them to feel superior.

Another reason people make fun of others is that people often make fun of people or things they don't understand or are afraid of. That's why there are so many ethnic jokes. You know the jokes I mean—the ones that start "How many [fill in the blank]s does it take to screw in a light bulb?" or "How do you get a [fill in the blank] to . . ." or "What does a [fill in the blank] say . . ." and others like that.

All of these jokes make fun of people simply because they were born into a particular race, part of the county, religious faith, or go to a certain high school—one that is different from ours.

We feel safe in our little culture and make fun of others who are from a different one.

That's wrong, and it's hurtful. What's important to remember is how it feels when you're the one being made fun of.

It doesn't feel too good, does it? Keep that in mind when you have the chance to make fun of someone else. Think about how it feels when you're on the receiving end. It hurts.

So why hurt others when you could turn it into an opportunity to help them feel better about who they are? You'll end up feeling better about yourself too. When you respect others, everybody wins and nobody loses.

That's one way to feel good.

Jesus understood about being put down. Lots of people made fun of him. It even happened when he was dying. He hung on a cross to save the world, and the people who gathered around to watch him die made fun of him.

"If you're really God's Son, why don't you save yourself?" they taunted. The Bible never tells us whether or not it bothered him. We do know that he resisted the temptation to fight back and insult them. He prayed for them instead. I think there's a lesson there for us.

There isn't any good reason for people to make fun of other people. They just do. The thing you need to do is remember the hurt such teasing can cause. Also remember how Jesus dealt with it.

Perhaps by acting the way Jesus did—praying for others instead of insulting them—you can help put an end to some of the teasing you know goes on at your school. You'll at least be stopping the teasing that you do.

If you do, I guarantee you'll end up feeling better about yourself than Rufus and Carla do at the expense of other people. You'll make God happy in the process too.

Respecting others is the mark of a real winner.

22

XXXXXXXXXXXXXXXXXXXXXXXXX

Who Invented Grounding?

The first written record of grounding is found in the *Odyssey* by Homer. No, not Homer Simpson! I mean the Greek writer of antiquity. No, that doesn't mean he wrote stories about old furniture! It means he wrote stories a long, long time ago—before your parents were born, even.

I've read this story a time or two and have always had a hard time understanding it. About the only thing I've figured out is it seems to be about some Greek kid who took some "victuals," according to Robert Fitzgerald's translation (with drawings by Hans Erni, which are almost as hard to understand as the written word). I have figured out that "victuals" must be Greek for "food." He then started off on a journey.

Along the way, the kid had all sorts of adventures that many teenage boys would like to have (beauteous damsels and dastardly villains and the like). He eventually came through it okay.

Not everyone else fared so well, however, and, so far as I can tell, the mythical Greek goddess Athena, upset that they had disobeyed her, grounded a whole bunch of them. Permanently—by putting them in the ground. About six feet deep. Dead, like.

This is the first known written example of grounding.

As you study great literature, you will find that the *Odyssey* is in the genre (that's French for "type") of literature known as tragedy.

I doubt that you have to be told what a tragedy being grounded is.

Grounding has been elevated to an art form by modern American parents. That's because around four thousand years have elapsed since the time Athena grounded the Geeks, uh, I mean Greeks. Today's parents have had a lot of time to improve on the original idea.

It's more challenging to ground someone nowadays than it was then too. In the old days, grounding was a relatively simple thing. You told someone to go to his or her island and stay there.

He did. It wasn't much fun. How could it be? There wasn't anything to do on the island except exist. Being grounded on an island in the Mediterranean Sea might sound pretty good to you, but remember, beach volleyball and bikinis hadn't been invented yet. AGT (Ancient Greece Time) was not a good time to be grounded.

As civilization advanced, and the world ran out of islands to ground teenagers on, parents had to become more creative. Time strode on and so did revolutions in grounding.

By the 1890s parents were grounding kids on their farms. There were chores to do, and even if they did wander around outside, they wouldn't see anyone other than one of their twenty-seven brothers and sisters or some of the assorted livestock. Back then, the nearest neighbors lived 4.7 miles away across the prairie.

In the language of the day, grounding was known as being "planted."

"Jimmy, did I hear your pa tell my pa that you and Laddie were planted for a month for tippin' over Old Man Pierson's outhouse—with Old Man Pierson still in it?"

"Yep, Johnnie, that is quite true."

Then, as civilization marched on (actually it caught a cab in 1911, shortly after the Model T had become such a hit, bringing with it the phenomenon known as a shrinking world), people began to discover their neighbors now lived next door rather than next county. This presented a new problem for parents. It meant they had to ground kids in the house to keep them from socializing.

Then, to make matters worse from a parent's perspective, came the advent of electronics.

When Marconi—no, not Macaroni, that's Italian pasta. I'm talking about Marconi. He's Italian too but he's just *pasta* history, not *pasta* you eat. Anyway, when Marconi, Edison, and others invented radio, records, and television, it suddenly didn't do much good to ground a person in the house.

With all those electronic devices, you could stay at home and still have a fairly lively social life. You could keep up with the adventures of Lamont Cranston, also known as "The Shadow" ("Who knows what evil lurks in the hearts of men, the Shadow does!") or revel in the adventures of "Sky King" ("From out of the blue of the western sky comes—Sky King," followed closely by his lovely niece, Penny.)

So parents began grounding kids in their rooms. After all, the only things they could do up there were study or sleep. Yea, rah!

Then came transistors and microchips and portable radios and TVs and VCRs and Walkmen and Watchmen, and now you almost have to pity parents who ground kids. Why send Lisa to her room? She's got more to do up there than her mom did on a date twenty years ago.

As a result, parents have had to get inventive, and inventive they have become.

Instead of grounding their kids in their rooms, I know parents who ground their kids from television, youth group, the car, cassettes, CDs, and their own rooms. Or worse.

"If you mess up one more time, young lady, you'll never go in your room again! I'll ground you in your brother's room."

"No, Mom, please. Anything but that sweat sock-infested swamp."

Grounding isn't the worst thing that could happen to you. It might seem that way at the time, but that's because you're not looking at it creatively. Use your imagination. Spend the time you are grounded doing things you normally wouldn't do. Read a book. Write a letter to a friend. Catch up on all your back homework. Find lost things in your room. Talk to God.

God knows all about grounding.

You see, the first known record of grounding wasn't really in the *Odyssey.* It was in the Bible.

Adam and Eve messed up (big time), so they got grounded and couldn't enter the garden and enjoy all the good stuff they had there. Instead of making them stay in the Garden of Eden, God, sounding a lot like the parents of today whom I mentioned earlier, made them get out.

That wasn't because God was such a bad guy. He made the rules, and he told Adam and Eve what the rules were. He did what he did because Adam and Eve knew the rules and broke them anyway. Sounds kind of like they might have been teenagers, doesn't it?

So God grounded them. He did it to give them a chance to think about what they had done and get right with him. Grounding can do that for a person. It makes you focus your thoughts on why you got grounded. After you get over being mad about it, the injustice of it all, and everything and start thinking about things, you can usually figure out why you got grounded in the first place. Then you decide what you are going to do about the situation. Are you going to sulk or resolve to not screw up again? If you are smart, you immediately decide the latter—to not screw up, at least in that particular way, again.

Yes, grounding has a long and rich tradition. Every parent does it. Even though now you say you won't, someday I'll bet you'll ground your kid. I know I do mine, just like Daddy grounded me.

Use the time wisely, learn from it, and grow. Make it work for you instead of against you.

Besides, it's a nice change of pace and a chance to get out of doing stuff you don't want to do anyhow.

"Go to Mrs. LaPorte's and rake leaves? Sorry, I can't. I'm grounded."

Added note: I just got grounded. Yesterday, just after writing the answer to this question, I went outside to play basketball with our son Tim. After shooting a few hoops, I went to pick up the ball and felt a sharp prick inside my middle finger. Something had stung me.

I had my first allergic reaction to being stung—and so spent the next three hours in the emergency room of our local hospital, hooked up to a heart monitor and getting treated like a pin cushion. All this in an effort to slow my heartbeat, help me breathe, and get rid of the nasty red blotches that covered my body.

It wasn't much fun.

Because of all that, today I am running a fever and am grounded. I had big plans for today too. I was traveling to another town to play in a softball tournament. But Dr. Dan, my medicine man, said, "No way."

I could mope. I could cry it's not fair. But I already told you to make the best of being grounded, so I'll take that advice.

Instead of driving to the hills of Brookville on this sunny fall day, I'm going to sit at home, watch some football on TV, and write to you. That's not my first choice, but it's still a good one.

I'll bet today will turn into an even better day than the one I had planned.

23

XXXXXXXXXXXXXXXXXXXXXXXXXXXX

Why Are Shoes, Watches, and Clothing So Special to Everyone?

Are you asking why people wear shoes? And watches? And clothing?

The answers to these questions are reasonably easy ones. People wear shoes so their feet won't get torn up by the terrible terrain over which they must travel—on the days they can't get rides, that is. Also, you never know what got pitched on the kitchen floor, and there is nothing worse than stepping on the soggy cornflakes the twins, Justin and Justine, spilled there and neglected to clean up, unless it is treading on the prongs of a dropped fork. These are all reasons why people wear shoes and think they are a nifty invention.

The main reason kids think watches are special is a watch lets them know just how many more minutes of school they have to endure. Surviving class time is high on a junior-higher's list of long-range plans, so watches help them mark their progress on that particular goal.

People think wearing clothes is special because, well, they cover up your—I mean it's so people won't see—oh, as a junior-higher you ought to be able to figure out this one on your own.

Now, if you are asking why do Nikes, Adidas, British Knights, LA Gear, Swatches, Lees, Levis, Jordache, Guess?, and other brand-name shoes, watches, and clothing items seem so important to people, that's something else indeed.

Why are the brands you wear so important? Problems arise when only a certain kind of shoe, watch, or clothing is "acceptable." We are not talking here about what your parents consider "acceptable." After all, so long as your clothes are neat and clean and match, parents don't care what you wear. It doesn't matter to them that it is last year's (or last decade's) fashion.

"It fits, doesn't it?"

("Yes, Mom.")

"And it looks good on you."

("Sure, Mom.")

"Who cares what the other kids are wearing?"

("I do, Mom.")

Of course, your part of this conversation is silent. It goes on only in your brain. You, as a wise child, do not question your parents' wisdom so far as clothes go. You have learned over the ages that they will buy what they want to buy and if you argue with them, they will buy it anyway and then immediately leave the store. If you suffer silently, they may relent and buy you something you really like. Then you can take all the stuff home, put the stuff they bought you in a bottom drawer (never to be seen again), and wear the things you like until they wear out.

Parents don't care what you wear, and they have a hard time wondering why you do. They have certain guidelines for purchasing things like shoes, watches, and clothing. These rules are handed to them at the hospital, within three minutes of your birth. It's the law.

Let's take a look at how those guidelines work.

Say you tell your parents you need a pair of shoes. The regulations they have to follow tell them that they have to help you pick out something sturdy, sensible, and economical. These are the three primary prescripts they have to follow.

We are going to take a look at the definitions of these words now—at least, what they signify to parents.

Sturdy means the shoes should be made of some indestructible material—like tiles from the space shuttle or your aunt's popcorn balls. Comfort is not a consideration here. Longevity is what counts.

To a parent, buying shoes for a teenager is similar to buying tires for the family car. *I wish I could find some shoes for that kid that were made out of the same stuff as those tires I got from Sears,* thinks Dad. *I got sixty-five thousand miles out of those dudes. Even Burt couldn't wear out those babies.* Your dad is going to get you something *you* can get sixty-five thousand miles (or two years—whichever comes first) out of. That's what sturdy means to him.

Sensible means you could wear the same pair of shoes to every function you would ever attend, except maybe to church or to run track. Parents think a kid needs only three pairs of shoes—"school shoes," "play shoes" (so you won't mess up your school shoes), and "dressy shoes."

"You should be grateful you've got three pairs of shoes," Dad says. "Why, when I was a youngster, I had only one pair of shoes, and they had to do me for everything. And I was grateful to have them. We were so poor that. . . ."

At that point, you begin to doze off because you know this is where he is going to ramble on and on about how tough it was when he was a kid. You've heard it all before—about how his family was so poor that all he ever got for Christmas was a new pair of jeans, a flannel shirt, a pair of shoes from PicWay Self-Serve ShoeMart (two pairs for five dollars), and a non–battery-powered machine gun, and that the sixteen members of his family shared a refrigerator carton in the middle of the road for a home—with another family.

You should be happy with sensible shoes.

Finally, there's *economical.*

Your mom thinks your shoes should not cost any more than whatever she earns in an hour at work. Parents don't think they need to spend a week's wages on something that goes on *your* feet. *Hey*, thinks Mom, *my shoes cost only $13.50, and I work for a stockbroker. Why should Michele who just goes to O.C. Moore Memorial Junior High School wear shoes that cost more? Who is she trying to impress?*

To you, your parents' three words are code words. They do not hold the same meaning for you as they do for them.

You know that *sturdy* means uncomfortable and unbearable. *Sensible* means ugly, uncomfortable, and unbearable. And *economical* means cheap, ugly, uncomfortable, and unbearable.

The rules we looked at for shoes hold true for the way parents feel about watches and clothes. They just don't know how important these things are.

They do seem to be important, don't they? Everyone at school places a lot of significance on them. What you wear on your feet, wrist, or body can determine which crowd you run with. You know you are going to have to dress a certain way if you want to be part of a certain group.

As much as you may hate to hear it, parents aren't entirely off the mark in their ideas on this subject. True, they may have taken it a bit too far, but they do have the essence of the idea right. What they have gotten right is that clothes, watches, and shoes do not turn you into somebody you want to be or make you over into somebody you are not. You are who you are, no matter how you dress.

Kids, at least many of them, haven't learned that yet. They put a lot of emphasis on how a person looks and what he or she is wearing. Parents care more about how a person acts.

For the only time you may remember, your parents are right. Even God agrees with them. You see, Jesus told people it was more important how they acted then how they looked. In fact, he told one group that was far too concerned about their appearance that they were like real fancy graves. On the outside they looked nice, but inside they were full of nothing but dead people's bones. Not a pleasant picture, is it?

What Jesus was saying was that what really matters is how you are on the inside. It is far more important to dress up your heart and soul than it is your body.

Dressing a heart isn't always easy. How do we know what to wear? The Bible gives us lots of clues. It tells us to dress up with love and kindness and gentleness and a whole lot of other things. Dress up this way, and people won't be paying as much attention to what you are wearing. Do the things you know are right, and it won't matter how you dress.

How you dress is important to people at school. What your heart is like is important to God. Which of the two would you rather impress?

24

✗✗✗✗✗✗✗✗✗✗✗✗✗✗✗✗✗✗✗✗✗✗✗✗✗

How Old Was the Oldest Person Who Ever Lived?

According to the Bible, a fellow by the name of Methuselah lived to be nine-hundred and sixty-nine years old. And you think being a teenager once is tough. Just think, he was a teenager when he was 118, 216, 313, 414, 515, 616, 717, 818, and 919. I wonder if he had zits each time and if his parents kept grounding him every time he messed up.

25

✗ ✗

Why Don't Parents Let You Sleep over at a Friend's House on School Nights?

Most adults would be greatly surprised to learn that this is one of the more pressing problems facing teenagers today. Many grown-ups think kids are more socially aware than the teens of years gone by. You think you are too, but your definition of *socially aware* and theirs are two different things.

For adults, being socially aware means being troubled by the larger issues of life on this planet. They think you are concerned with deep problems—things like toxic waste, the greenhouse effect, the global economy, and so on. They believe you are consumed with worries about your future.

You, on the other hand, think being socially aware has to do with your social life. So, it's a disappointment to many adults to discover that your social awareness mostly involves problems like this one—and the future that concerns you is the next fifteen minutes instead of the next fifteen years.

So let's take a look at this problem of modern teendom.

You and Pat have been best buddies for years. You really enjoy spending time together. In fact, if you could, you would spend all your time together. This is hard to do since you live in separate houses seven blocks apart. So you scheme to overcome this teenage time/space continuum (a scientific dilemma expressed in the formula $(X_1 - Z^{23}) \times [9,2365.5 > 1^{721053}] = 0$, which means a good friend times a different house equals not enough time spent together).

Your solution, young Einstein?

"We'll spend the night together," you reply. "That way we'll be together from the time school is out today until it's time for school to start tomorrow."

Uh-oh. There's the problem. Two problems, actually. School and tomorrow. You know what your parents are going to say. You don't even have to bring up the subject. You would barely get the question past your lips before your mom would say, "Not tonight, dear. It's a school night, you know."

Yeah, I know, you think, *so what's the point?*

Of course, you are wise enough not to vocalize anything even remotely resembling that thought. Following that line of reasoning will get you nothing but grief and the third degree on where you got such a smart aleck nature: "It certainly wasn't from me. Why, if I had talked to my mother the way you just talked to me, I would've been lucky to sit down for a week. And that's after Mother got through with me. Then it would've been Dad's turn. Why, I tell you . . ."

That and another hour-and-a-half oration on the subject of "the point." Which is, as you also already know, "because I'm your parent and I said so" and hardly worth another ninety minutes of your time. (Do you know what an hour and a half is in teenager years? It's almost the equivalent of three decades for a fifty-year-old!)

But while that may be the point, it's not the real reason your mom won't let you spend this Wednesday night at Pat's house. If you think about it, you can figure that out yourself. The real reason is contained in the answer to the following question: When you spend the night with a friend, do you sleep?

Sleep? Sleep! You've got to be kidding. There's no way you get any sleep. The purpose of sleeping over is to stay up as late as you can talking about anything you can. Yes, it may be called sleeping over, but everyone knows that *sleeping* is the wrong word.

Parents know this. Yes, even yours. How? Because, though it is almost inconceivable to you, your parents were once kids. When they were teenagers they stayed over at their friends' homes (I know this is almost too much—first they were young and now I'm telling you they had friends). When they stayed over, they didn't sleep. They remember that.

That's how they know that if you go to Pat's house, you will arrive at around 3:30 in the afternoon or so and at 3:30 in the morning you'll still be up talking about Indianapolis' chances in the Super Bowl or the Cubs in the World Series or Kristi and Jeff and Kathy and David and Steve and Bonnie and Pfenninger's new stereo, and on and on and on.

That's the real reason your parents won't let you sleep over—because you won't sleep.

"So we won't sleep," you say. "What's your point?"

You can say this to me because I'm not your parent. I can't give you the Look (you know which one I mean) and lecture you for an hour and a half. Since I am a parent, I'll get to the point. I'm going to do it by asking you a question: When you go to school on an average day, do you ever feel sleepy in class? Like maybe every class, every day?

That's the point. If you are sleepy on a normal day, why compound the problem? If, on the best of days, after all the rest you get at home (it's so boring there you go to bed early, don't you?) you still feel sleepy in class, why add to the problem?

After you've spent the night getting all the juicy details on all the couples in junior high, you are not going to be in any kind of shape to even *act* as if you're paying attention in class. Nope. It's hard enough on a regular day. There's no way you'll be able to keep your eyes open.

You are certain to find yourself sitting there with your eyes glazing over and the stuff on the blackboard running together and then your eyes shutting and you snoring and coming to with Mr. Newby standing over you saying, ever so politely, of course, "I'm so sorry. Am I keeping you up?"

All this time, you thought your parents made that rule because they thought you would stay up all night and go to school the next day and not learn anything.

News Flash! News Flash! They know you go to school a lot of days and don't learn anything. Some of that could stem from an attitude we all have had, which is, "I don't feel like being here and they can't teach me anything today." Other times, it's for other reasons.

The reason your parents made that rule is to keep you from getting in trouble. Surprised? I thought you might be.

See, your parents don't want you to get in trouble. Mom and Dad really want the best for you. It's true.

Parents want their kids to do well. They want them to succeed and get through life with a minimum of hurt and pain. Sometimes parents help by saying yes, other times by saying no, not to be mean but to aid teens along the way—to help them avoid some of the pitfalls in life.

That's a lot like the way God does it. God has set up rules about how we are to live, things we are to do and things we aren't. These rules are not meant to be mean and stifle our fun. Instead, they are to keep us out of trouble.

That's why God made the rules. He set them up, knowing that if we followed them, our lives would be easier, richer, and less painful. Life can be tough (kind of like school). God tries to make it easier on us. If we follow God's rules, things that deal with not lying, stealing, hurting others, and so on, we won't always be worrying about how we are going to get out of "this" mess—whichever one we are in at the time.

God made rules because he loves us. Remember that, and do your best to keep them. For your sake as well as his.

So, enjoy sleeping (ha!) over at Pat's on the weekends. And fake being awake during the week.

Most of all, thank your dad for making sure you won't be waking up in class, with Mr. Newby staring you down.

26

✗✗✗✗✗✗✗✗✗✗✗✗✗✗✗✗✗✗✗✗✗✗✗✗✗✗✗✗✗

How Can You Say "Shut Up" to Principals?

You can't and live to tell about it.

27

✗ ✗

Why Is Gym So Hot and Sweaty?

It's so you know you are in a gym and not a classroom. Everyone knows gyms are supposed to smell bad. If they didn't, you'd think you were in English class instead of gym class, wouldn't you?

28

✗ ✗

How Do You Meet Girls?

I don't. At least, not on purpose. You see, I'm not allowed to. Nancy, my wife, has very strong feelings against my going out and meeting girls. It has something to do with already being married and wishing to stay alive.

Besides, I like and love her. I think she's the neatest girl I ever met, so I don't really want to meet any others. Nobody else could compare with her in my eyes and heart.

If what you want to know is how *you* can meet girls, perhaps I can answer that question too. Please remember, though, I am just telling you how to meet girls. I am not going to be putting these ideas into practice myself.

The first thing you need to do is make a list. On it, you want answers to the eternal question, "Where can girls be found?" Or to rephrase the title of an old Elvis Presley (he was a rock-and-roll singer from the olden days) movie (which can be seen all the time on some cable stations' "Long Live 'The King'—a 72–Hour Cinematic salute to Elvis Aaron Presley") "Where Are the Girls?"

To help you get started, here's the beginning of a list:

1. School
2. Church
3. The mall
4. At a friend's house
5. In their own homes

This initial list is a good beginning, but it's too general. It needs to be broken down more. You need to make it more specific. To do that, ask questions like *where* at school, the church, the mall, and so on. Then your list will begin to look like this:

School	Church	Mall	Friend's	Own House
Homeroom	Worship Service	Clothing Stores	Amanda's	611 Stewart
Home Ec class	Sunday School	Clothing Stores—	Mary Pat's	Drive
Girls' Gym	Youth Group	Dressing Rooms	Charlotte's	
Girls' Gym Locker	Youth Group Car	Clothing Stores—	Laurel's	
Room	Wash	Checkout Counters	Ashley's	
		Shoe Stores	Whitney's	
			Audrey's	

Second, review your list. Which of these are places you could go or things you could do to put yourself in the same places as girls and meet them?

You also need to make a list of places you can't or shouldn't go. Again, to help you get started, I'll make a few suggestions. Avoid the girls' gym and girls' gym locker room and clothing store dressing rooms.

You could go to these places and you would probably meet girls—but you'd also meet the school principal, store manager, and arresting officer as well.

Carefully mark the good places with an asterisk (*) and the bad places with nothing. Do that just so you won't get confused and forget whether * meant good or bad and end up at the wrong place at a very wrong time.

Now your list should look something like this:

School	Church	Mall	Friend's	Own House
*Homeroom	*Worship Service	*Clothing Stores	*Amanda's	*611 Stewart Drive
*Home Ec class	*Sunday School	Clothing Stores— Dressing Rooms	*Mary Pat's	
Girls' Gym	*Youth Group	*Clothing Stores— Checkout Counters	*Charlotte's	
Girls' Gym Locker Room	*Youth Group Car Wash	*Shoe Stores	*Laurel's	
			*Ashley's	
			*Whitney's	
			*Audrey's	

After reviewing your list of places where girls are that you can be too, rank them in order of acceptability. Acceptability means presenting the best possible circumstances for a positive meeting.

For example, while it may seem that meeting her at her home is acceptable, it might not be. Yes, you are allowed to be there without having the police called, but it might not be acceptable because her dad doesn't like your type (a boy) hanging around his precious little girl. I know Nancy's dad felt that way (and maybe still does) about me.

Take these kinds of feelings into consideration, then number your list by level of acceptability. Consider 1 very good and 5 very bad.

How do you meet girls?

When you are through, your list should look something like this:

School	Church	Mall	Friend's	Own House
2. Homeroom	2. Worship Service	1. Clothing Stores Clothing Stores—Dressing Rooms	3. Amanda's	5. 611 Stewart Drive
1. Home Ec class	1. Sunday School	4. Clothing Stores—Checkout Counters (might end up paying for something)	3. Mary Pat's	
Girls' Gym	1. Youth Group		3. Charlotte's	
Girls' Gym Locker Room	5. Youth Group Car Wash		3. Laurel's	
			3. Ashley's	
			3. Whitney's	
		1. Shoe Stores	3. Audrey's (You can never tell what will happen at her friend's house)	

Then go to those places you've marked with a 1. This will be especially helpful if, for example, you signed up for Home Ec. Not only will not showing up mean you won't meet girls, it will also mean you flunked another class. This is something you definitely don't need.

Home Ec is a really good place to meet girls. It is better than the mall because at the mall, girls and guys hang around different places. Besides, girls don't have to talk to you at the mall. As a matter of fact, they probably won't. They might talk *about* you but not *to* you.

Home Ec is a much better choice, for a number of reasons. First, girls are impressed by any guy who acts secure enough in his masculinity in a class that has a history of being primarily for girls.

"Gee, I'll bet Brett's really sensitive."

"Yeah, he's so sweet. The rest of the eighth-grade guys are taking auto body shop and getting all grungy and sweaty, and he's here hemming a shirtsleeve."

Second, you can talk in lots of Home Ec classes. This is a real plus. Can you think of many classes where this happens?

No! In every other class, the teacher is telling you to shut up.

In Home Ec, freedom of speech abounds. Classmates converse freely, exchanging recipes, clothing patterns, ingredients, and the like.

You can talk to girls while meeting them, instead of just staring longingly, the way you do in English class.

Finally, many Home Ec projects require partners. You can try to come up with a way to get Rachel to be your partner. That means she'll have to work with you, which means she'll have to talk and spend time with you.

Taking Home Ec is one of the easiest ways for a teenage boy to meet girls.

There is another place on the list. It's one you might not have thought much about: church. It's too bad you haven't thought about it, and awfully shortsighted. You see, there are lots of churches across this great land of ours. Lots of girls go to them. Churches provide opportunities to meet these girls. You can meet them at scheduled services, youth group outings, in Sunday school classes, lots of places.

There's good news about meeting girls at church. It's easy. All you have to do is go there. The girls you meet there will be pretty special. They'll know that there's more to life than who you are. It's more *whose* you are. If they know they are God's they are learning to live lives of joy, peace, goodness, and other soul-fully satisfying things. Trust me, you could do a lot worse then meeting one of these girls.

Of course, you have to be on your guard. While meeting girls at church, you might meet someone else—God. You know that God is everywhere, but he hangs around churches a lot. That's where a lot of people go to meet him. So, go to church and meet girls. Meet God there too. You could make it kind of a spiritual double date.

29

✗ ✗

How Do You Make Friends with Boys?

This question seems to follow naturally the one be-fore. In answering each one, I have made an assumption about both. That assumption is that the first question was written by a boy, and this one was penned by a girl.

How I, or any other male-type person, make friends with boys is going to be different from the way a girl would. What I am trying to say is that boys make friends with other boys in different ways than girls make friends with boys. Boys most often make friends with other boys by playing the same games as they do. We play basketball, football, baseball, Risk, Monopoly, tennis, Ping-Pong, or anything that has an edge of competition to it. If a boy gets hot and sweaty doing it (which is usually not very appealing to girls and other humans), well, that's even better.

The only way to top it is to blacken another guy's eye, break his nose, or drive his teeth through his lips and bloody them good. If this happens, you can count on the two guys being friends for life. Don't ask me why. I don't know. It doesn't make any sense. In that way, it is a lot like life. There's no logic to it, but that's the way it is.

Playing games against guys won't work for many girls, for a number of reasons.

First, ask yourself if you really want to get hot, sweaty, bloody, and smelly. Chances are you don't.

That's one reason it doesn't work the same for girls as it does for guys.

Second, guys, especially the younger they are, don't like to be beaten. At anything. By anyone. Ever. They especially hate being beaten by a *girl*. Yes, this is sexist. It's antiwoman. It's not politically correct thinking for the nineties. But it's true. And it remains true even when guys get older. Oh, they may hide it better, but even to the ones who act as if they are sensitive and it doesn't matter, trust me, it matters.

Junior high guys just haven't learned to hide their disgust at being beaten by females. That's one of the main differences between boys and men.

It's just plain hard for girls to make friends with guys in junior high. That's because guys don't want to be friends with girls until they want to.

Confused? So are they. This one is complex. It all depends on the guy or the group he runs around with.

Some guys want to be friends with girls as early as preschool days. Others are in their mid-thirties before they decide whether or not this is a good idea.

And guys tend to hang around other guys who are just like them. So, if the guy you want to be friends with hangs around a band of buddies who think it is extremely uncool to be friends with a girl, well, I don't know how to say it except, "Look for another guy to be friends with."

It's pretty discouraging, isn't it? Actually, it's not that bad. Becoming friends with a boy is a lot like becoming friends with a human being. It helps to have some of the same interests. If he likes cars and sports and you like cars and sports, then it's easier.

Whatever you do, don't fake it. Guys can tell if you don't know a 16-valve, 4.2-liter engine from a 16-ounce or 2.0-liter bottle of Pepsi. Besides, you'll soon get tired of acting as if you care about something you don't.

If you want to make friends with a guy, begin by making two lists. Sounds familiar, doesn't it? That's because I like lists, and they can be helpful.

On one list, write the things you like to do and are interested in. Then make a list of guys you'd like to be friends with and things you think they'd be interested in. The finished product might look something like this:

me	Rob	Mike	Brian
music—modern	music—heavy metal	music—all kinds	himself
books	all sports	movies—funny	himself
movies—funny and sad but not too sad	food	books	himself
cats	food	cats and dogs	himself
most sports	food	football, tennis, golf	

Go over the lists. Compare them. Then strike up a conversation with Mike, the guy whose list most closely matches yours. This may sound scary, but it's really easy, for a couple of reasons.

First, you won't have to worry about what the guy is going to say. He'll be so surprised you talked to him first, he probably won't say anything. The element of surprise has won a lot of battles—and the battle of the sexes is no different.

Second, he'll be so flattered, he won't know what to do. I'm not kidding. Guys find it hard to believe a girl

105

would want to be friends with them—especially someone as great as you. Guys spend a lot of time trying to get up enough nerve to talk to you—so much so that, if you talk to them first, they'll be so floored, flattered, and flustered, they'll be positively appreciative.

After all, you've taken the heat and pressure off them. What teenage boy could ask for more?

Even if they aren't flattered, that's their problem. They don't know what a good thing they just missed out on if they don't want to be friends with you.

There is one guy who does want to be friends with you, and you'll want to make sure you're friends with him too. His name is Jesus. Jesus can be every girl's best boyfriend. If you are looking for a friend who will never lie to you, will always be there for you, and is a good listener to boot, then Jesus is the Friend for you. He does all that, for a lot of people, and he wants to do that for you too.

There are lots of boys to meet out there. Some of the ones you thought were really neat will turn out to be jerks. Others you thought were nerds will turn out to be Prince Charmings.

Regardless, Jesus is the one guy who is always the same as he appears. He's kind, sensitive, caring, and very much in love with you. You can be introduced to him lots of places. You can meet him at church, a Young Life or Campus Life Club, summer camp, or in the quiet of your heart.

If you haven't already met him, do so today. He's the best friend, male or female, you'll ever have.

30

✗ ✗

Why Does It Seem Like You Always Get Stuck with the Bad Teachers?

Because you do.

31

✗ ✗

Why Is It in Junior High, if You Tell a Secret but Tell Your Friend Not to Say Anything, It Always Gets out Somehow?

Do you want to know a secret?

You do? Okay, lean down real close to the page. No, closer. You've got to get closer. You see (or you hope to, anyhow), I'm going to write it really, really small so no one else can see it.

It's something between you and me. It will be so small that nobody else will be able to read it. Just you. And you've got to promise not to tell.

The secret is: There's no such thing as a secret.

What's that? You say it was too small to read clearly? You didn't get what I was saying? Well then, let me repeat myself a little more boldly.

The secret is: There's no such thing as a secret.

There just isn't. You and I both wish there were. You may think that just because you can, and do, keep secrets, everybody else will too. It doesn't work that way. This is especially true the older you get. Some people love to hear juicy, secret things. They want to know the scoop on everything. They want to be privy to personal information. Yes, they really enjoy hearing secrets. But not as much as they like telling them.

Even the great philosophers Lennon (John Lennon, not Lenin of Russia) and McCartney of a long-ago group called The Beatles knew people had a hard time keeping secrets—even boyfriends and girlfriends. They once asked:

> Listen, do you want to know a secret?
> Do you promise not to tell?
> Let me whisper in your ear
> Little words you want to hear.

John Lennon and Paul McCartney knew that people want to know secrets but they knew you have to make them promise not to tell. They also knew that, even if they do promise, they will probably still tell. Why? As much as I hate to say it, it's human nature. That's just the way we are. Yes, I said *we.* You and I are included in that group.

Lots of times we say things we shouldn't. Somebody has told us something about someone else, or themselves, and we have promised not to tell. And we really meant it. We do okay at it for a little while. A few days, even. But then, when we have let down our guard, someone says something close to the secret and we find ourselves blurting out, "Yeah, and then he went and. . . ." "And . . ." Right about there, we become aware that we've just let slip what we promised to take to our graves with us. It wasn't because we want to hurt our friend. It was just that it was too hard to keep inside. It's hard not to tell stuff we know. It just slips out.

Of course, there are some people who delight in letting secrets "slip." I said it that way because they don't really "slip." They know all along that they are going to tell somebody what they have heard in secret, especially when it sounds really scandalous. Some people just like to tell everything they know.

I know a guy who knew lots of things that should have been kept secret. Things were told to him because of his job. They were things that, because of his position, only he was supposed to know, and they could really hurt people if they got out.

They got out a lot. Too much. Many people got hurt. Lots of times I would hear him say to someone, "Listen, between you and me, and in the confidence of these four walls, let me tell you about . . ."

Telling even one person who wasn't supposed to know anything about secret situations, even "in the confidence of these four walls" was bad enough. But he didn't do it just once. He did it all the time. This guy told the same "secret" stuff over and over to many different people—all of it "in the confidence of these four walls."

A lot of folks finally quit confiding in him. Others avoided him. Some quit talking to him altogether. And he wonders why—and keeps telling secrets.

Most of us aren't nearly as bad about it as the guy I know, but it's still hard to keep our mouths shut when we know something secret. We like to echo the old school yard chant, "I know something you don't know!" Then we go ahead and tell what we know.

Though you may not believe it now, it doesn't happen only in junior high. It happens all through life. There are only two ways to be sure your secrets don't get out. One is not to tell anybody anything you don't want repeated. Keep your secrets to yourself.

The second is to tell them to somebody you can trust to never say anything about them. Not even a word. There's only one Person I can think of who fits that description totally. That's God.

You can tell God anything and sleep well knowing it won't get out. Whatever you want to say will be between just the two of you. Not a word will ever get out.

God does want to know your secrets. Well, actually, God already knows them. What he likes is for you to talk to him about them firsthand, not because he enjoys juicy gossip or anything. It's because he enjoys talking to you. He wants you to feel easy around him. Easy enough to trust. Easy enough to tell your innermost feelings.

You can also be assured that when your best friend is talking to God, God won't say to her, "By the way, do you want to know what Lauren told me today?"

After all, it's a secret.

32

✗ ✗

Why Do Teachers Have to Be So Weird?

It's the law.

33

✗ ✗

Why Do We Have to Dress Up for Church When We Are Told That God Loves Us for Who We Are, Not How We Look?

You may be among the people in this world who think that the Bible is nothing but a bunch of rules and regulations. And I must admit, it does have its share of them. The best known of these are the Commandments and the Golden Rule, all of which can be summed up as, "Do unto others as if you were one of the others."

In spite of that, I didn't think there were any rules in the Bible about having to dress up to go to church. I wasn't sure, though, so I did some checking. To my surprise, I found there were some rules about dressing. Like the one in Deuteronomy 22:5, which says, "A woman shall not wear anything that pertains to a man, nor shall a man put on a woman's garment; for whoever does these things is an abomination to the Lord your God."

Besides which, a man in a dress generally looks pretty silly.

Then there's Leviticus 19:19, "nor shall there come upon you a garment of cloth made of two kinds of stuff," which I take to mean that you should avoid synthetics like polyester, since it's made from a bunch of chemicals and who knows what else. And it looks tacky too.

To me, both of these rules seem to have a lot more to do with how a person should dress appropriately than they do with dressing up for church.

So I searched some more. *After all,* I thought, *perhaps there is some dressing up in the Bible.* I remembered a story about Joseph's coat of many colors. That must have some implications about dressing up.

It does, but they are not good ones. The coat was made for him by his dad and didn't do anything for him but get him into trouble with his brothers. They weren't too happy about his being Dad's favorite in the first place.

I think that tells us dressing up too much isn't such a good idea.

Proverbs 31:22 (KJV) talks about the ideal woman: "She maketh herself coverings of tapestry; her clothing is silk and purple." Even though her clothes are fancy, she makes them herself. She doesn't buy them at that French clothier, *Jacques Penney.* But it doesn't say whether or not she wears them to church.

According to the Bible, John the Baptist wouldn't win any marks as a sharp dresser. The passages about him say he wore a coat of camel's hair tied with a leather belt. He sounds like the original hippie.

As I looked, it began to appear that the Bible didn't have any commands about dressing up, either to go to the market or to church. As a matter of fact, the Bible even warns against people who dress up for church. Jesus told his followers to beware of the scribes (religious bigwigs of the day) who "like to go about in long robes."

He didn't mean borrowed bathrobes like the ones you wore in the second grade when you were a wise man in the annual church Christmas pageant. He meant you shouldn't dress up for church to impress the other people there. The scribes dressed that way to call attention to themselves. They thought it made them look more "spiritual" than the other people.

Jesus goes on to say we shouldn't worry about what to wear: "If God do clothes the grass of the field, which today is alive and tomorrow is thrown into the oven, will he not much more clothe you?" (Matthew 6:30). What I think he means is that we shouldn't worry too much about dressing up in the latest fashions or buying them at the best stores. The type of clothes a person wears doesn't seem to be too important to Jesus.

That's not to say the Bible doesn't say anything about how we are to be attired. It's just that the clothing the Bible is concerned with is the invisible sort— soul clothes.

The Bible tells us what this kind of clothing is. First Peter 5:5 says we should be clothed with humility. Isaiah talks about the garments of salvation and the robe of righteousness.

For all my searching, I couldn't find anything like, "Before thou goest to church or Sunday school, thou must put on thy finest clothing," or, "When thee headest out for worship service, be sure thy clothes are new and neatly pressed so that thou willest impress the Lord thy God."

No, when the Bible talks about what we are to wear before God, it has to do with those already-mentioned invisible, spiritual clothes and not with something new from the mall.

So how come you have to dress up to go to church if it's not in the Bible?

115

That has more to do with people than it does with God. You see, it's one of those rules people made up. Church people are good at making up rules that don't have a lot to do with the Bible. The people making them up think they come from the Bible, but that's because following these rules makes them feel that they're closer to God than others who don't follow their made-up rules.

Down through the ages, people who follow God have made up new rules that have nothing to do with his original ones. As a matter of fact, by the time Jesus came, the simple rule about honoring the Sabbath and keeping it holy had turned into about 467 rules about just how that was to be done.

Jesus turned it all around. He turned all the many rules into two: Love God and love your neighbor. That's the way he said all the rules could be summed up. But those who have followed him since have tried to add new rules. They say Jesus didn't fill in enough information. He didn't mean to, of course, but he left out important stuff about what makes you a Christian—stuff about how to dress, whether or not to wear make up, dance, go to movies, roller skate, go to circuses, and lots, lots more.

I guess they know more about being a Christian than Jesus does. At least they think they do. I wish I could tell you to ignore all these people's rules because God doesn't care. I wish I could, because it's true. God doesn't care a whole lot about the externals. He does care about how you clothe your life and heart. He doesn't worry too much about the clothes that cover your body.

116

Your parents and others do care, though. At this point in your life, they exercise a lot of say over how you dress and other parts of your life. That's not to say it's right or wrong, it's just the way it is. Someday it will be entirely up to you how you dress for church. You know it doesn't matter to God. What matters is whether or not you show up at all.

For now, as much as you hate to dress up, do it anyway. Turn it around. Don't think of it as having to dress up for God. Think of it as dressing up for the people who think that's the only way to get ready for God. It's important to them.

If you want to dress up for God, then take out your heart and polish it up a little. Then those "dresser upper" people and God will both like the way you are clothed for church.

34

✗✗✗✗✗✗✗✗✗✗✗✗✗✗✗✗✗✗✗✗✗✗✗✗✗✗

Why Can't You Use a Calculator on a Test?

Because they don't want you cheating in history class.

35

xxxxxxxxxxxxxxxxxxxxxxxxx

Why Are Parents So Strict on Their Kids These Days?

Parents get strict because there are a lot of temptations in the world. There are plenty of things calling out to all of us, trying to get us to do things that are harmful to us.

We are surrounded by advertisements for evil. I know that sounds harsh. It sounds like something a parent would say. Regardless, it's true. TV, movies, magazines, and music are all filled with things contrary to the Christian life—things like having sex with anyone you want whenever you want, getting drunk or high, cheating on people, stealing, murder, and crass materialism. That last one means having everything just because you want it. Buy, buy, buy, buy, buy. Take, take, take, take, take.

If you think I'm exaggerating, just watch an hour of television and then write and tell me how many times you were glad during that hour that Jesus wasn't sitting on the sofa watching with you. How many times would you have been embarrassed if he had been there?

Besides what we get in the media, some people we hang around with want us to do stuff we know we shouldn't—like "have a beer, my folks are gone for the night," or, "Eric stole a copy of the answers for tomorrow's algebra quiz—want a copy so you don't have to study?"

That's just the people we know. Our friends. Then there are people we don't know. They want us to get as screwed up as they are. Junkies who would love to get us hooked on drugs, not because drugs have made their lives better but because if we buy drugs from them, they get money from us—so they can buy more drugs. It's a business deal, not something between friends.

Your parents know all this. In addition, your parents were kids once—long, long ago, in a galaxy far, far away. But still they were kids. They remember how hard it was for them and parents being the gloomy sorts they often are, they are convinced the world is tougher and more full of temptation now then it was when they were young. So they are strict because they want to protect you.

That's an insult, I know. After all, you don't need protecting, do you? You can handle yourself. You know the difference between right and wrong, good and evil. And you always choose wisely.

Your parents hope you do. Deep down, they even know you'll try. Yet, because you are a kid and human, every now and then you mess up. Maybe not on the big stuff. It's not as if you are out stealing cars or anything and are going to get sent to the Watchoochie Boys' School. But you mess up on small stuff, like missing a curfew or forgetting to do that science project you've had three weeks to work on. So your parents worry and get strict and try to run your life.

Sometimes they try to make themselves feel better by setting rules they think will help you stay out of trouble—not that they think you are out looking for it, but rather that it is out looking for you.

Believe it or not, parents care. They want the best for you. They want to help you, not mess up your life. I know it doesn't seem that way. They seem to do a lot more interfering than is necessary. That's part of being a parent—messing in your kid's life. You'll understand this better when you are a parent.

Try to be patient with your folks. They are learning to be parents while you are learning how to grow up. You see, there was no license required before they could become parents. There were no classes they had to take or tests they had to pass. Well, other than a pregnancy test. But that was the only one.

Then all of a sudden, they end up with a screaming, squalling you. They feel overwhelmed with joy—and the burden of helping you get to adulthood. It's scary. It stays scary.

Parents always wonder if they are doing the right thing. Should they have said this? or done that? or taken you here? or let you go there? and on and on and on.

A good way for you to live through this period is to be accepting of this need they have to be strict. Show them you can be trusted and that you understand why they think rules are necessary. Even if you don't.

36

XXXXXXXXXXXXXXXXXXXXXXXXXX

Why Can't Peer Pressure
Be Stopped and Everyone
Just Act Like Themselves?

Are you sure that's what you want? Do you really want everyone to act the way they want? Even Freddy Krueger or Jason? I'm not sure you do.

Peer pressure has gotten a bad rap. Peer pressure is not always bad. Sometimes it's even good.

Before we take a look at why it can be good, we have to first take a look at what it is. Peer pressure is nothing more, or less, than the pressure other people our own age, social rank, educational level, or other stuff put on us to behave a certain way. Peer pressure takes many forms. It affects us all.

You may not think of them this way, but laws are a sort of peer pressure. Our peers, in this case all other humans, put pressure on us to not commit murder, rob convenience stores, and mug little old ladies. Laws are a kind of codified (written down) peer pressure. They are an out-in-the-open sort of peer pressure. You know they are there and what's expected.

There are more subtle kinds of peer pressure. One is the kind that says if you behave in certain ways you'll be accepted (or at least tolerated) by a certain group. The behavior varies from group to group, but the peer pressure is there, whether it is by fellow basketball team or gang members. Some of this is bad. Some of it is good.

It can be good when it makes the kid who is constantly disrupting class and getting everyone in trouble to cool it. You know the kind of peer pressure I mean. It's when every student in the class turns an icy, straight-to-the-heart stare on that kid in the third row after he's gotten everyone awarded an F on the pop quiz because he was such a smart aleck.

That's the last time he'll do that. And live.

Just think—Freddy Krueger and Jason might have turned out better if their peers had put a little pressure on them. That's the good kind of peer pressure.

Of course, there's lots of negative peer pressure too. That's the kind that is worrying you. It's the peer pressure that says you have to dress, act, and do certain things before you're accepted.

Since you want to be accepted, you give in to the peer pressure. Instead of being an individual, you become part of the crowd. Many times you do this while saying you are doing it to assert your individuality.

For example, your parents hate your new haircut. So do most other adults. That's because it's not like their haircuts—or they don't have any hair at all (a fact in which teenage boys take certain evil delight). How do you reply?

"I got it cut that way because I'm an individual."

This, in spite of the fact that every other kid in school has a haircut just like it, and you got it so you would fit in better.

There's our choice—to be part of a good crowd where each member can still think as an individual, or sign up to be part of the Lemming League. Don't bemoan good peer pressure. Be aware of the bad stuff.

And thank God you're a teen with enough brains to make good choices, and not a lemming looking for a place to drop into.

37

✗✗✗✗✗✗✗✗✗✗✗✗✗✗✗✗✗✗✗✗✗✗✗✗✗✗

What Is the Use of School?

It gives teachers a place to go during the day. If it weren't for school, teachers would spend their waking hours wandering the streets, trying to stay out of trouble.

38

✗ ✗

Do Parents Ever Have Fun, or Do They Even Know the Meaning of the Word?

Yes, parents have fun. It's not the same kind of fun you have, but they do have fun.

Parents' fun is similar to yours, I guess. I mean, fun is fun. Everyone, even parents, knows what's fun and what's not. It's not too difficult to tell the difference between fun and not-fun.

Fun is enjoyable; not-fun is not enjoyable.

Eating your favorite food is fun. Eating brussels sprouts at the Reverend Dr. J. Stanley Bankerblood's house is not fun. Even parents will agree to that.

I guess I've answered the second part of your question first. Yes, parents do know the meaning of the word *fun,* at least so far as its basic definition goes. It's in the expanded amplification that something gets lost in the translation in the transition from adolescent to adult.

Put another way, like in everyday English, what I mean is, though parents and kids agree on the basics of what fun is, it's in each group's larger definition of *fun* that the difference becomes apparent. And I do mean "a parent."

To a kid, fun is active. To a parent, fun is passive. For kids, fun is usually something you do. It's like,

Do parents ever have fun, or do they even know the meaning of the word?

"Let's go play miniature golf, cruise Broad Street, and stop by Brad's. That'll be fun."

For a parent, fun is something that happens to you. "Gee, Janie, that TV show sure was fun."

If you have been the least bit observant as an adolescent (child, kid, teenager, or whatever), you will have noticed your parent(s) becoming less active. He or she tends to be living in slow, then slower, motion. Speed has gone from gazellelike to glacierlike. Dad tends to watch sports on TV instead of playing them at the school yard. Mom tends to shop by catalog instead of malling, as she used to.

You, on the other hand, are constantly on the go. You have deep physical, psychological, and emotional needs that keep you on the move. They go away as you get older. Fun for you is going somewhere, doing something with someone. For your mom or dad, it's surviving the day.

You want to TP someone's house, they want to watch TV at someone's house. You're in the middle of the crowd at the football game, and they are at home trying to figure if they can pick you out of the crowd on the telecast of the football game. You go to the Dead Pet Shop Girls concert and they sit in their LaZBoys listening to a CD of Johnny Mathis.

You see, it's not that they don't have fun or know the meaning of the word, it's just that your definitions are different.

The bad news is that, as you get older, your view will become more like theirs instead of theirs becoming more like yours. As bad as that is, it's not the worst thing that could happen. That would be if they did change their definition to be the same as yours. You know what I mean, don't you?

Every now and then, some poor teenager gets parents who realize they are getting older and they try to fight it. They start dressing like their kid, talking like their kid, and acting like their kid. It's so embarrassing. Adults are supposed to be adults and stay on their side of the age fence. Everyone knows that—except these parents.

I haven't met a girl yet who wanted her mom hanging out at the mall with her. Or any guys who wanted their dads out playing "21" on the basketball court with their buddies on a daily basis.

Every once in a while is okay, or at least tolerated. But all the time? No thank you. Let kids be kids and grown-ups be boring.

Be grateful your parents are aging as gracefully(?) as they are. Say a prayer of thanks each night that they aren't trying to hold back the tide of years by becoming your best buddy and driving you out to TP someone's house or going with you to see *Bill and Ted's Most Excellent, Bogus, Gnarly, Totally Outrageous, Stupid Adventure Part III*.

Yep, kids should be kids and adults should be adults—and stay that way.

The Bible tells us that when we grow up we put away the things of our youth. That doesn't mean the things of youth were bad. They weren't. It's just that they aren't appropriate for when it's time to be an adult.

The way a person has fun is one of those things that gets put away or changed. Your parents have learned that and gone on to more adult things. That's the way God meant it to happen.

Enjoy your type of fun now, and let your parents enjoy theirs. As confusing as it may be, since the two seem so different, don't worry too much about them not knowing the meaning of the word. They do. It's just that it wears them out thinking about it.

39

XXXXXXXXXXXXXXXXXXXXXXXXXX

What Is So Important about History?

Nothing. It's just that if there were no history, there would be no present, so you wouldn't have a future. That's all.

40

✗✗✗✗✗✗✗✗✗✗✗✗✗✗✗✗✗✗✗✗✗✗✗✗✗✗✗✗✗✗

How Do You Fit All Your Stuff in Your Locker?

I don't have this problem any longer. You see, I haven't had a locker for almost . . . well, you really don't need to know how many years it's been since I've had a locker. It's enough for you to know that the only guys my age who still have lockers probably also hold the record for being the oldest active players in the NFL. So I don't have to worry about fitting all my stuff into my locker. My problem now is how do I get everything into my briefcase?

Which points out something interesting. Well, I think it's interesting, and since I'm the one writing this book, you're going to read about it whether you want to or not. Unless of course you skip the next page or two.

Well, hurry up, make up your mind. Are you going to read what I have to say or not? I haven't got all day here. (Do I sound like a parent? I thought I might.)

The interesting point I want to make is this—problems don't necessarily change when you get older. They just change focus.

One of the problems that has plagued every human who has ever lived is where are you going to put your stuff? This problem affects everybody, no matter what age.

It all began a very long time ago. Adam and Eve, during the time they obeyed God, got to live in the

Garden of Eden, and they were the only humans who didn't have to worry about it. That's because they didn't have any stuff. They didn't need any closets to hang clothes or put their shoes in. There wasn't any clothing.

But Eve got the ball rolling by inventing fig leaf clothing.

Incidentally, Eve came up with a saying that women have passed genetically through their side of the species: "I don't have anything to wear." In her case, though, it was true. All of a sudden, she and Adam had stuff and nowhere to put it. God created the world and everything in it, but he left it up to humans to create a need for closets. From that time on, humans have had stuff they needed to store. It's all Adam and Eve's fault.

This need begins when you are young. Very young. Like when you are born. From then on, you need a place to put your stuff (diapers, sleepers, pacifiers, and other baby stuff), and it's a dilemma trying to figure out where to put it all.

As you get older, you acquire more things. As a kid, you have toys. If you are the first child in your family (and especially the first grandchild), you have lots of toys. You need a place to put them. So your parents give you a place. Most likely it's a closet or a dresser drawer. Some kids even have toy boxes. It doesn't matter how much space you have, it's never enough. Your possessions never seem to fit. Stuff is always spilling out of your space.

When you're older, you start school and get a desk. That's okay the first day or two. Then, like the toy box before it, stuff like pencils, papers, paste, and scissors start spilling out all over the place.

Next it's on to junior high. When you get there, the school grandly gives you a locker. This is great. A locker of your own. It's huge—lots bigger than a desk.

There's more room here than I could ever fill up, you think. Wrong. As you have already discovered, it's hard to fit all your stuff in that tiny space.

I want to be helpful. To ease your space problem let me give you a list of what you should put in your locker. If you stick solely to the stuff on this list, it will fit. I promise.

Stuff That Goes In:

Books

Your coat or jacket (just one at a time, please)

Notebook

Lunch (if you carry one to school, not the one from the cafeteria, with a tray and all)

While you may disagree that this is stuff that should go in, it is what the school administration had in mind when it designed and gave you a locker. That's why it's so small.

Now let's look at what you're trying to put in your locker. This is what makes it impossible to put in the necessary stuff (see above list):

Stuff That Doesn't Have to Go In:

Gym clothes that have been used three weeks in a row

Last week's lunches you forgot to eat

Ice cream

Every pop quiz, test, and page of homework that teachers have handed back to you since you started junior high

Your ten best friends' stuff

Your boyfriend's/girlfriend's stuff

Stuff you don't want to take home but it's too valuable to throw out (like one piece of gum, a broken compass, *Mad* magazine)

Other magazines

Overdue books

Three changes of clothes

This list could go on, but I think you get my point. There's enough essential stuff you need to put in a locker without adding anything else.

Life is like a locker. There are lots of things clamoring for space in the locker that is your life. You have to decide what to put in there and what to leave out. This is a tough decision.

Once again, here are some lists.

Stuff to Put In:

Love

Kindness

Gentleness

Goodness

God

Family

Friends

Stuff That Shouldn't Go In:

Well, you're smart enough to figure out what shouldn't go in. You don't need my help there. Just remember, like your locker at school, your life has only so much room. Choose wisely what you're going to fill it with. Get rid of the stuff that is doing nothing but cluttering it up. Leave enough room to add stuff that will make it nicer. An air freshener might help your locker. Air freshener might help your life too. The best air freshener there is comes from God's Spirit blowing throughout your life. He helps you keep the right stuff in there too.

41

✗ ✗

How Come When One Grade Goes Up, All the Rest Drop?

Though you probably have not studied much physics yet (since it's a subject you will try to pass in high school), you are probably aware of an English chap named Newton and his famous discovery.

No, not the Fig Newton. That was discovered, I mean invented, I mean baked by Nabisco.

I am talking about Sir Isaac Newton and his discovery in the area of physics. Newton is the guy who got bonked by an apple falling off a tree and that one hit on the head induced all sorts of discoveries. He wrote these down in a little book titled *Philosophiae Naturalis Principia Mathematica.* You might want to check it out for a little bedtime reading someday.

One of his most well-known discoveries was what goes up must come down.

What is not so well known is that his son, Isaac Newton, Jr., or little Newt, as he was known to his friends at Queen Elizabeth I Junior High School, came up with a corollary to his father's famous principle. "What is a corollary?" you ask. "I know what a coro*nary* is. It's what my dad has when he sees my report card."

Well, a corollary is something that naturally follows something else. Understand? I didn't think so. I'm not sure I understand either. But what affects you is Newt's corollary, which is—and he discovered this back in 1666, remember—when one grade goes up, another must go down.

He wrote his findings in a book entitled *Flunkingus Classis Inus Philosophiae Naturalis Principius Mathematica.*

Now do you understand why, when one grade goes up, the others go down? It is a law of physics. It is nothing you have any control over. It is just something that happens.

Yes, you may spend lots of time raising that C in Spanish to a B, only to watch sadly as your A in Algebra slowly sinks in the west. It's natural law.

You begin each grading period with new determination to make all A's. *How hard can it be?* You think. *I'm pretty close already. I had only one B last time . . . and one C and one C-. I can do it.* So you really go to work in Spanish. You take extra interest in math. You turn in all your art class assignments on time. And you get all A's—in Spanish, math, and art. Of course, your A's in English and social studies are now a B and C, respectively.

Why? Because of little Newt's corollary! That and the fact that you were probably spending so much time on Spanish, math, and art, you let English and social studies slide. After all, you got A's in them last time. They were covered. So you didn't worry about them.

You probably didn't have to worry about them, but it wouldn't have hurt to have studied them some, along with Spanish, math, and art.

Life is that way sometimes. We give ourselves report cards all the time.

Hey, you think, *I got an A in etiquette, but I could have done better in helping out around the house and need major improvement in cleaning up that trash pile I call my bedroom.* So for the next few weeks, you spend a lot of time cleaning up your room and forget to say "please" and "thank you" when you should. When one personal grade went up, two or more went down.

That happens in our spiritual lives sometimes too. You think, *I'm really going to work on praying and reading my Bible.* And you do. But then you forget to help someone who really needs it. You were too busy memorizing the Sermon on the Mount to be living it.

What's the point? The point is, don't worry about slipping grades. It's something that happens. Just keep working on bringing them all up slowly. Let one grade sneak up on another. Pretty soon it will catch up. Let your B sneak up on that A and surprise it, before it has a chance to fall.

Do that in life too. Try to get a little bit better every day in all areas of life. Don't knock yourself out in one area, only to neglect the others. Strive to be well rounded and good at lots of things.

As far as your spiritual life goes, begin praying and reading your Bible while continuing to live out your faith the way you always have. If you do that, you get all A's there too.

42

✗ ✗

Why Do Teachers Tell You to Go Look It Up in the Dictionary When You Don't Know How to Spell It?

This is a question that has bothered junior-highers since the beginning of the student/teacher ratio. The first recorded instance of its being asked out loud was when Plateau (Plato's little brother) asked Socrates, "Oh, wise teacher, how do you spell *truth?*"

To which the great philosopher replied, "Look it up in the dictionary."

At that point, Plateau said, "That's stupid. How am I going to look it up in the dictionary if I don't know how to spell it? How do I know where to begin looking? If I knew how to find it in the dictionary, I would already know how to spell it, and I wouldn't have to look it up in the dictionary, would I?"

That's when he decided being a philosopher was going to be a lot more work than he had planned on. He didn't want to spend the rest of his life running between Socrates and the dictionary looking up *life, beauty, love, wisdom,* and so forth.

"So, wise Brentcrates," you ask, "why is it that teachers, philosophers, and other adults tell you to go look it up in the dictionary?"

And I reply, "There are three answers to this philosophical question, my child."

140

Well, actually, you're not my child. In most cases, I don't even know you personally. But it sounds like something a great philosopher would say.

The first reason is that teachers want to cover their own ignorance. They don't know how to spell the word. Instead of letting you find out that they can't spell *stupid,* they tell you to go look it up. It takes the heat off them.

The second reason is that it's a genetic defect afflicting all adults. It's something over which they have no control. It is a medical fact that when a person turns twenty-one, a gene (just recently discovered in the hippopotamusatomusthylus—the part of the brain that governs the spelling of names of large land mammals) suddenly clicks on. When it does, it forces the adult to reply to any young person who asks a spelling question, "Go look it up in the dictionary."

You see, it's not their fault. They can't help themselves. Their brains make them do it.

The third and perhaps most important reason is they want to enhance your research skills. Adults think you should learn how to use books from the reference part of the library. You know, the big ones that the librarian won't let you check out—encyclopedias, dictionaries, thesauri, atlases, and the like. These are all materials you will need to use as (and if) you progress through your educational experience.

When you use them, you learn lots of things. For example, using a dictionary helps you learn how to spell correctly. But a dictionary doesn't just show you how to spell good—or well, even—it also tells you lots of things about words. Good dictionaries show you a word's origin, usage, and meaning.

141

By opening a dictionary, you not only learn how to spell, you also learn other things about the word you're investigating. That's the point of the trip to the dictionary. By using it when you don't know how to spell something (or anything), you end up learning other things as well.

Maybe you should try doing the same sort of thing when you want to find out about God. What I mean is, there are lots of people who will tell you all about who God is, what God is like, and what part God should play in your life. Much of it is good, and all of it is well intentioned.

But just as someone telling you how to spell a word doesn't really help you learn much about the word, someone telling you about God doesn't really help you get to know him. Unless you look into God yourself, all you have done is gathered secondhand information. It is all someone else's opinion. All you know about God is what you've been told. It's not what you've discovered on your own.

If you want to know what God is like, look him up. No, not in the dictionary. It's easier than that. You can begin by reading the Book he gave us. It's all about God and his interaction with humans. It tells how he communicates with us, what he wants us to do, how he's helped us out of jams in the past, and how much he loves us. His Book is called the Bible, in case you were wondering.

Do you need another way to look God up? Here's one that's even easier than the first. It's by talking to him. That's right, just talk to him. That's one of the exciting things about God and your relationship with him. You have lots of ways to find out all about him.

You can do that yourself. You don't have to rely on somebody else to find out what God is like.

Others, such as pastors, Sunday school teachers, youth leaders, parents, and friends, can be sources to draw from. They can teach you a lot. But ultimately, it's between you and God. You get to know him by yourself. You don't need anybody to pave the way for you. God's door is always open, and all you have to do to visit him is to walk through that door. You can go to God direct. That's the best way.

43

✗✗✗✗✗✗✗✗✗✗✗✗✗✗✗✗✗✗✗✗✗✗✗✗✗

Why Do There Have to Be So Many Problems Growing Up?

Problems? What problems? How can you have any problems—you're just a kid. You may think you have problems, but buddy-boy, you don't have a clue about what problems are. Just wait until you're an adult and have mortgage payments, car payments, credit card payments, a lousy job, a grouchy boss, a . . .

Does that sound like most adults when you mention the problems you have? Adults are good (or bad, depending on your point of view) at belittling your problems. They act like yours are so unimportant measured against theirs.

In that respect, adults aren't very different from anybody else. Everyone thinks the problems he or she is facing are real problems, while the stuff other people are dealing with is minor in comparison.

The thing a lot of people forget is there is no such thing as a problem that isn't real to the person having it. Problems don't become *real* problems just because a person turns thirteen or eighteen or twenty-one or forty. We have *real* problems all of our lives.

For example, when you are first born, there are three things that are real problems for you. The first is getting food into your tummy. You don't know why that's important, but you do know that your tummy hurts when it gets empty. So you want food.

The second is getting the food your tummy didn't want (and so passed on to another part of your body, which then passed it on to a diaper) off your bottom. It smells bad and is uncomfortable. You want to be cleaned up.

The third is getting enough sleep.

Since babies can't talk, you make your intentions known by crying. This gets annoying after a while, both for you and anyone else who has to listen—but especially for the older brother who just got chewed out and sent to his room for writing on the newly painted living room wall.

He looks at the baby—you—and says: "You think you've got problems. All you have to do is lie around, sleep, eat, and poop. I'm the one with problems. I have a room to pick up, I'm in trouble for writing on the wall, and next year I have to start going to school and doing homework and stuff."

Meanwhile, his older sister is saying: "You think you have problems. What's going to happen to me when Mom finds out I ran a stop sign in her car and got a ticket? And that instead of going to the movies with Therese I really went with Don. And that I still haven't finished my math homework—from last week."

And Mom says: "You think you have problems. My car broke down and I can't afford to get it fixed this week. The rent is due tomorrow, and I don't get paid till next week. My credit cards are all charged up. I need to put your grandma in a nursing home . . ."

Everybody has problems. Everybody's own problems are the biggest and most important to them. Which doesn't really answer your question, except to let you know that growing up isn't special just because you have problems. I wish it were, but it's not. Nope. You're going to have problems all your life.

That's a cheery thought, isn't it? You were probably hoping this was another one of those phases your parents are always telling you you'd better outgrow (and praying you would). But it's not. Problems are with us always.

That's the bad news. The good news is there is someone you can tell your problems to. Someone who will listen and understand and help you through them. That's God.

God is intimately interested in your problems. Not because he wants to gossip about them (*see* my answer to the question about keeping secrets) but because he wants to help. God has a record of helping people survive and overcome their problems. He wants to help, if you'll let him.

While I wish I could tell you that you're soon to outgrow having problems, you won't. You are always going to have trials and tribulations. The important thing is to not let your problems get you down. They will come and go. You can, and will, outlast them. There is no problem so big that you can't overpower it. Just ask for some help from your family, friends, or church.

God's there when you need him too. All you have to do is call.

44

✗ ✗

Why Do Parents Punish Us for Things They Did When They Were Kids and Thought It Was Funny When They Did Them?

That's because when *they* did them, it *was* funny. When you do the same thing, you are being a stupid, immature, reckless child.

You see, as you get older, your perspective—your view of the world—changes. As you become an adult, all the things you did as a kid and thought nothing of now crowd into your brain. You see all their potential danger, and you think, *I'm lucky to be alive.*

Some people are. Lucky to be alive, that is—especially after all their teenage activities.

When you are a kid, you feel nothing can harm you. Bad stuff happens to other people. Other people fall off roofs, get in car wrecks, or break their necks playing football. Nothing like that is going to happen to you. This world holds no fear for you. No evil—except for teachers and parents—will ever befall you.

You think you are sort of immortal. Sure, you know you could be killed in a car wreck or some other accident. You know it intellectually, that is. But you don't really accept that something like that could happen to you. It just couldn't.

When you are a kid, accidents and death are things that happen to somebody else. Not to you. When you are an adult, getting really old and beginning to reflect on your past life (this happens around age thirty or so), you come face-to-face with your own mortality.

When you're that old, suddenly death seems right around the corner. It is then you have your primary indication that your life, as you now know it, will end sometime. You realize you are not going to live forever.

That's when you think about the stupid stuff you did as a teenager. And when you think of those things and remember some of the simpleminded stunts you pulled as a kid, you realize it's a miracle you're still alive.

Since you are alive, you look back on those things and laugh. They seem funny because you cheated death and disaster. You climbed billboards on the edge of town. You and your buddies played hide-and-seek in city storm sewers. And nobody, except you and your buddies, knew about it.

There is lots of other stuff too. Stuff nobody knows about. Especially not your parents. Even as an adult, you don't want them finding out about all the nonsense you did.

When you are old and get together with old friends, you begin to reminisce about the days of yore and the years of living dangerously. The conversation somehow takes you out of the stodgy, stifling workaday world you live in, and you find yourself transported back to the days of your youth—days of great fun (*see* earlier question on fun) when you were

INVINCIBLE!

You were, as long as your parents didn't find out, anyhow. Not that you should hide things from your parents.

That's where the problem is for you. You'd be better off if your parents didn't remember those days. When they do, they see them in two ways: fun for them and dangerous for you. That's because they also remember how lucky they were to survive all those things. They want you to survive too. So they go nuts whenever you pull something they once did—and thought was funny.

It's a double standard, I know. It's not fair. I've got more bad news for you. Life isn't fair. That's just the way it is.

There's one set of rules for parents, another for kids. The really unfair thing from your point of view (as a kid) is the group that gets to set the rules. That's the parents.

What you need to learn to do is accept that tragic fact. Just because you hear your dad laughing himself silly while visiting with some old friends and recalling the time he sneaked into the teachers' lounge, lifted a toilet seat, and stretched Saran Wrap across the toilet right before old Mr. Shore walked in to use it—well, don't plan on doing it yourself.

Their laughter is not a clue that this is a good idea.

For one thing, what many adults forget, while caught up in their marvelous memories of misadventures, are the times they got caught and had to pay the consequences—because they usually did get caught. Old age has just erased that part of their memory tape.

You'll get caught too if you try the same stuff.

Yes, you may learn great things from your parents. Things you should emulate and put into practice yourself. Pranks, however, are not on that list, and if you try any, you'll find that out.

It doesn't always pay to follow your parents' example.

That's true of your earthly parents. It's something else again when it comes to your heavenly parent.

You can always trust God. The example he sets is always a good one. He has never pulled any mischievous stunts that, if you try them, will end up getting you in trouble. In fact, just the opposite is true. If you do what God would do in a particular situation, you'll end up not getting in trouble at all.

This would be hard for you, I know. It's hard for me. It's hard for any human. But it is what God wants us to do—to become God impersonators. To imitate his actions—actions full of love, caring, kindness, and gentleness toward others.

So, enjoy your earthly parents' stories of impishness and mayhem, but don't imitate them. At the same time, enjoy stories of your heavenly parent's activities. Try to imitate all of them.

45

✗ ✗

Has Algebra Ever Saved Anyone's Life?

You may find it hard to believe, but the answer is yes. Algebra has saved someone's life. The story of how it happened is not well known. As a matter of fact, this is the first time it has ever been put on paper.

Once upon a time . . . well, let me start another way, or else you'll think it's a fairy tale.

It happened a long, long time ago. The entire earth was engulfed in war. Nation had risen against nation. The Axis powers (Germany, Italy, and Japan) were run by dictators who had enslaved their own people and forced them to work toward the despicable design of world domination.

These wicked warriors were well on their way to overrunning the entire world. Standing against them and their perfidious plans were the free nations of the earth, known as the Allies. These nations eventually triumphed and helped restore peace and order to all nations ravaged by the war. But our story takes place when the outcome was still very much in doubt. It looked as if the free nations would lose. Freedom seemed to be slipping away. It happened in the deepest, darkest time of the mighty conflict, the winter of 1942.

Nazi Germany had put a U-boat (submarine) blockade around Great Britain, cutting off that valiant island nation's supply of armaments, food, and perhaps most important, textbooks. All across the harsh English countryside that bleak winter, youngsters were suffering from lack of warm winter woolens, fresh fruits and vegetables, and reading material. The plight of these poor children was overwhelming.

Across the sea in the United States, caring people were hard at work raising funds so they could send convoys of ships laden with clothing and foodstuffs to their English "cousins." At the same time, a handful of educators realized that feeding and warming those little British bodies would be of little use if their minds were not given stuff to feed and warm them as well. They set about the task of raising money so a boatload of books could be sent along with the convoy.

But alas, their job was harder than they had thought it would be. People saw the need for food and clothes but often missed seeing how vital books were. The funds came in slowly. Too slowly.

The ships sailed without them. The dawn of January 12 saw a mighty convoy of heavily laden American merchant ships put out to sea, guarded by the best of His Majesty's Royal Navy. The protection of traveling under the watchful eyes of the battleship *Duke of Ellington* and the cruiser *Sir Loin of Beef* and their brothers in arms was to be denied to the boatload of books the educators wished to send.

Still, they went about their business with an ardor unsurpassed in the annals of Anglo/American education. Working with textbook publishers and fellow teachers, they raised the necessary funds, secured a ship, and coaxed a crew to take her, alone and unprotected, across the "Big Ditch," as the Atlantic Ocean was known in those war-torn years.

They chose a fine ship manned by stalwart sailors. It was the SS *Lee King Tubb,* commanded by Captain Carl and his valiant crew of merchant marines (Terry, Teddy, Neil, and Bubba). They set off after dark on the evening of January 13. Steaming at full speed in hopes of catching the convoy and the protection that lay therein, the ship traversed the treacherous seas of the Straits of Nova, through the Bay of Bisquick, and across the windswept, wave-tossed North Atlantic.

For three long days (some of them lasting twenty-seven or twenty-eight hours) of high seas, wet snow, cold rain, high heat, and humidity, running in the face of a Force Nine gale, the tiny ship was tossed. If not for the courage of the valiant crew, the *Lee King* would be lost. The *Lee King* would be lost.

Then, when it seemed they would never make contact with the convoy, Bubba, from his vantage point high in the *Lee King's* crow's nest, shouted, "Hey," which the rest of the crew knew meant the convoy was in sight. Protection was at hand.

Then tragedy struck.

Unbeknownst to the crew of the *Lee King,* they had been picked up on the ultrasensitive radar of the mighty Nazi battleship *Weinerschnitzel.* The *Weiner-schnitzel* had secretly put to sea the same night as the *Lee King,* and with a full array of the best the Nazi navy (*Der BootzendenGermanische*) had to offer, had steamed westward to catch the convoy. Somehow, to the *Lee King's* misfortune, the *Weinerschnitzel* had missed the convoy entirely and zeroed in on it instead.

AdmiralsunderBoztsendenGermanische Herbkersman was enraged that they had missed the convoy. He had been sent along as commander precisely so the convoy could be smashed. In anger, he ordered the mighty guns of the *Weinerschniztel* trained on the hapless *Lee King*. He also transmitted a secret signal to Kaptianer Schmiesser, commander of the German submarine fleet of the North Atlantic (*Bunchen den Boatens datgoinsUnderderWater*), ordering him to fire at will—or at the *Lee King*, whichever came into range first.

At precisely 12:01:01 A.M. on January 17, the night sky was lit up with salvo after salvo of shots from the *Weinerschnitzel*. Shells the size of small town houses flew across the trackless wastes of the sea, wending their way on their deadly mission, at last finding their mark. All were direct hits on the *Lee King Tubb*.

At 12:01:02 A.M., Schmiesser and his wolf pack of U-boats fired 147 torpedoes, also scoring direct hits.

Debris from the tiny ship flew into the air and rained down from the sky for almost two hours and thirty minutes. The Nazis sailed away.

When at last the roiling, boiling sea returned to some semblance of calm, a lone figure was seen bobbing on its surface, kept afloat only by the buoyancy of the books to which she was clinging.

It was Mrs. Hollingworth, a teacher who had stowed away on the ship. For four weeks she fought off sharks, dive-bombers, piranhas, thirst, *Brady Bunch* reruns, heat, barracudas, submarines, and cold clinging to those two books. At last, a convoy bound for New York to pick up supplies spotted her, hove to, and brought her aboard.

Down in the ship's hospital, the ship's surgeon put her gently on the ship's hospital bed and slowly pried the two books from her frozen grasp. They were copies of Shaffer and Medley's *Principles of Algebra.*

Mrs. Hollingsworth's first words upon regaining consciousness were, "Algebra saved my life."

What's the point? "Everything you write," you say, "has a point. Let's have it."

The point is—there is no point. I wrote this one just for fun. Maybe that's the point—that it is okay to just have fun.

You could even learn that lesson from the Bible. "Where?" you ask? Look at Psalm 119. It's the longest psalm in the Bible. There's a reason for that. The person who wrote it wanted to use every letter in the Hebrew alphabet, in succession, to start each verse. So he did.

In other words, even though he was writing a psalm to God, he was also having fun.

Now that I think about it, this story does have a point—a pretty good one too. It's okay to have fun. It's more than okay, even. God wants you to enjoy life, to have fun. God liked it enough to put some in his Bible. Follow God's advice and enjoy living.

Joy!